IN THE UNITY OF THE FAITH

In the Unity
of the Faith

Twenty-seven Sermons and Meditations

Foreword by Edwin T. Dahlberg

THE CHRISTIAN EDUCATION PRESS • *Philadelphia*

Foreword

✙ SOME YEARS AGO there was an editorial in *Fortune* magazine entitled "Preaching Still Gets Results." This statement might well be applied to those who have preached the sermons you are now about to read. They are people who have demonstrated the power to get results, both in their preaching and in their churchmanship.

The twenty-seven ambassadors of Christ whose messages are recorded here have all played a significant part in the ecumenical movement of the Christian church. Some are archbishops and bishops of their respective communions; some are presidents, stated clerks, or executives by other names. They voice the faith of churches all the way from the Eastern Orthodox groups to the Seventh Day Baptists and the Philadelphia Yearly Meeting of Friends. Yet they speak one language. The accents of the Man of Galilee can be clearly heard.

DR. EDWIN T. DAHLBERG, President of the National Council of the Churches of Christ in the U.S.A.; Minister of the Delmar Baptist Church, St. Louis, Missouri

This book disproves the theory that when ministers become administrators they lose the prophetic note. It may be true, as one cynic expressed it, that "even the prophet Isaiah would have learned a great deal if he could have spent three years as the pastor of the Old First Church in Jerusalem." But the distinguished churchmen and churchwomen whose sermons are included in this volume have not quenched the Spirit. They have learned much, not only from the local churches they have served, but from the wider denominational and ecumenical fellowship in which they have been such notable participants. This gives substance and reality to what they say. They are accustomed to preaching for a verdict.

It is good that the editors included the sermons not only of men but of women; not only of the clergy, but of the laity; not only of the white race, but of the Negro race.

It is fortunate, too, that the publication of this book coincides with the tenth anniversary of the National Council of the Churches of Christ in the United States of America. This event will be celebrated in the General Assembly of the National Council in San Francisco, December 4-9, 1960, and will have as its theme "Jesus Christ, Living Lord of All Life." All these sermons strike the ecumenical note. They make us conscious of "Christian responsibility on a changing planet." The unity spoken of here is something more than unity for its own sake. It is not a superficial "togetherness." It is unity with a passionate and powerful sense of mission. It is designed, to quote the words of the apostle Paul, to build up "the body of Christ, until we all attain to the unity of the faith and of the knowledge of the Son of God, to mature manhood, to the measure of the stature of the fullness of Christ" (Eph. 4:12b-13).

A dramatic scene was enacted at the laying of the cornerstone of the new Interchurch Center on Morningside Heights in New York City, October 19, 1958. Inserted into the main block of Alabama limestone was an ancient stone from the Agora in Corinth—a gift of the Greek Archdiocese of North and South America. Carved into this paving block from the first century A.D. were the words, "This stone is from the Agora in Corinth where 'many . . . hearing Paul believed.' " Thus the faith and doctrine of the New Testament church were placed squarely in the center of the science, learning, religion, and culture of the twentieth century, as a witness to all generations of the Christ who is "the same yesterday and today and for ever."

We are only forty years away from the morning of New Year's Day, A.D. 2000. The dawning of that day looms up before us like a rose-tinted mountain peak on the Millennial Divide, challenging us to explore the unknown passes of history that lead to the far frontiers of the Nuclear Space Age. Never was the church under such necessity to think in long-range terms concerning its mission to the nation and to the world. Men and women everywhere are asking searching questions as to the relevancy of the gospel. Is it still the good news of God in Jesus Christ, in a universe where just one little luminous patch in the distant skies represents the light of thirteen billion suns? What is the urgency and authority of the Word of God to men?

It has been my privilege to know personally most of the men and women whose sermons are included in the following pages. They are Christian leaders who have been "baptized into a feeling of the conditions of the people." Their preaching gives evidence that they have heeded the admonition of Karl Barth "to preach each Sunday morning as if that were the last Sunday in history."

May God bless all of us who read what they have written and spoken, that with the help of the Holy Spirit we may achieve the answer to Christ's prayer on the last evening of his earthly life: "That they may all be one; even as thou, Father, art in me, and I in thee, that they also may be in us, so that the world may believe that thou hast sent me. The glory which thou hast given me I have given to them, that they may be one even as we are one" (John 17:21-22).

Contents

IN THE UNITY OF THE FAITH

What Is God Saying to the Churches?

He who has an ear, let him hear what the Spirit says to
the churches.   —REVELATION 2:7a

✝ ON AN AUGUST AFTERNOON in 1959 I visited the rocky island of Patmos, which rises out of the wine-dark Aegean
Sea a few miles off the coast of Asia Minor. It was on this
island nearly nineteen centuries ago that John saw his visions
and wrote them into the Bible's last and climactic book, The
Revelation.

I visited the island in the company of representatives of
Christian churches from all over the world who, as the Central Committee of the World Council of Churches, had been
holding an annual meeting on the Island of Rhodes for the
preceding ten days. During our meeting we had heard
speeches from preachers and theologians from Germany and
Greece, from India and Britain, from Africa and the United
States. We had heard reports of several million dollars' worth
of refugee and rehabilitation work, and of continuing studies
on such diverse subjects as "A Theology for Evangelism" and

DR. EUGENE CARSON BLAKE, Stated Clerk of The United
Presbyterian Church in the United States of America

1

"Our Common Christian Responsibility for Areas of Rapid Social Change," and on "Religious Liberty."

We established a budget; we approved plans for the new headquarters' buildings in Geneva; we planned the world-wide strategy for the integration of the Missionary Movement and the World Council of Churches; we laid plans for the next World Assembly of the Churches in New Delhi, India, in 1961. Yes, our ten days had been filled with busyness about many things.

But at every World Council meeting there is one over-arching subject of concern: What is God saying to the churches? What word from God can we hear today for our strength and our salvation? There are two reasons why a committee or assembly of the World Council of Churches offers an especially good occasion for hearing what God may be saying to his church.

In the first place, the World Council takes the Scriptures very seriously. I suppose this is due to no special virtue on its part. The reason the Bible is studied so intently in the World Council of Churches is that amid the diverse Christian traditions represented there, from Friends and Salvation Army on the one hand to the ancient Eastern Churches on the other, all alike by the sharp variety of tradition are forced to look to the Scriptures which they have in common. I remind you that we Presbyterians, who are suspicious of the whole idea of tradition, have our tradition too. Confronted with other diverse understandings of the gospel of Jesus Christ, we along with others are forced to examine precisely what the Bible says, not taking for granted our fathers' interpretation, since the descendants of our fathers' opponents are there in the flesh to challenge us. In the twelve years of the World Council of Churches' life, churches of all traditions have found that a most creative way to mutual understanding is to examine the Word together.

In the second place, a meeting of the World Council of Churches is a good occasion to listen to God's speaking to the churches, since the highly diverse cultural, geographic, political, and economic backgrounds of the delegates clearly and quickly correct one's understanding of what God is saying. Here is an East German bishop of the Lutheran Church; here is the impressive Methodist secretary of the Council of Churches of newly independent Ghana; here is a Calvinist theologian from Czechoslovakia; and here, a new Hungarian bishop appointed since 1956 to take the place of an old friend of many years who is now in government disfavor. Also present are the most distinguished pastor of France, Marc Boegner; a bishop of the Church of England; a lay politician from Cincinnati; the president of Harvard University; a village preacher from Ceylon; and an erudite theological professor from South India. What a diverse lot of human beings, including me!

We have one thing in common. We represent churches which acknowledge that Jesus Christ is God and Savior. That is all that gives us unity. That is all that holds us together. But I testify that this common personal faith and allegiance does hold us together. And we are driven to ask on deeper levels, "What really is the God of all the earth saying to his church by the Spirit today?" And we help each other hear and understand. In that company we may not easily follow the universal shallow tendency to make God our patron only, with whom we soon become so intimate that we begin to patronize him.

So it was that all of us were ready to be thrilled as we visited the very place where John had seen his vision and written his message to the churches so long ago. We climbed the rocky road up to the ancient monastery where are lovingly preserved priceless ancient manuscripts illuminated by the artistic devotion of generations of pious men. Nearby we saw the cave where John, we were told, was living when he was inspired to write his book. This book of Revelation was written, you remember, after the first flush of enthusiasm for the new faith was passing, even though the church was still so very young. Persecution by the mighty forces of the Roman Empire was beginning to threaten the infant church. I am not at all sure that the cave we saw ever housed the writer of the book. But just to be there on the island where we know the book was written, to see the same blue sky and the same dark sea, to look across the narrow straits to Asia where the churches then were being born, to sense the age of the Christian church, and, in company with my diverse companions, to realize its variety, to be troubled at its weakening divisions, and yet to feel its unity in Jesus Christ—this made the visit a memorable experience.

So I suppose it was inevitable that I should preach a sermon on the theme, "God Speaks to the Churches," and choose my text from the book of Revelation: "He who has an ear, let him hear what the Spirit says to the churches."

How hard it must be even for God to speak to such a diverse lot as the churches of Jesus Christ, divided, rich, poor, radical, conservative, Eastern, Western. What can God say to his people in New York that is not contradicted by what he must say to his people in Tunis, or Texas, or on the borders of Tibet?

Yet this is what John attempted to do in the book of Revelation—to report what God by the Spirit was saying to *all* the Christian churches. As John looked across the straits from the heights of the island of Patmos, he saw in his vision seven of the churches in seven cities, all nearby. Seven has long been called the perfect number, signifying and symbolizing in this case all the churches—both those that existed then and all that exist today. Beginning in the second chapter of the book, John writes God's word to each of the ancient churches: Ephesus, Smyrna, Pergamum, Thyatira, Sardis, Philadelphia, and Laodicea. What he said to those churches was surely individually applicable nineteen centuries ago. Just as surely, the messages have a universal application to us. I shall not pick out one or more and apply them to one congregation, or to our whole church in America. I should hardly dare. But as I remind you in bare outline form of what God said to those churches long ago, I hope you will be sensitive to the Spirit to hear what God may be saying to us now. "He who has an ear, let him hear what the Spirit says to the churches."

The first is to Ephesus, the city where the great temple to Diana stood, and where, you remember, the preaching of Paul stirred opposition because it threatened the economic prosperity of the silversmiths' business of making idols to Diana, goddess of the hunt. Here as to most of the churches, God's word is one of both encouragement and warning. Let us thankfully accept every encouragement, if it applies truly to our church's life, and let us heed God's ancient warnings too. And surely it will be true that some of God's words of encouragement do not apply to us. Let us then be more ready to apply warnings to ourselves than, as the Pharisee, to thank God we are not as other men are.

To Ephesus, God said, "I know your works, your toil and your patient endurance" (Rev. 2:2a). He said, in effect, "You have been discerning amongst those who call themselves God's spokesmen, separating the true from the false." All this is encouragement. "But I have this against you, that you have abandoned the love you had at first" (Rev. 2:4). Let every church then be reminded that even orthodoxy, steadfastness, and labor are no substitute for the overflowing love that is a mark of every true company of Christ's disciples.

To Smyrna, God said, "I know your tribulation and your

poverty (but you are rich). Do not fear what you are about to suffer. . . . Be faithful unto death" (Rev. 2:9a, 10). Clearly we may not apply this to ourselves in this free land. But may we not as we hear this word remember, and identify ourselves with, our fellow Christians in China and Colombia, in Hungary and Romania, or wherever followers of Jesus may be called upon to be "faithful unto death," praying both for them and for their persecutors.

To Pergamum there was a different word of encouragement and a different warning. Its people had been through a persecution and had been faithful. Like Elijah, who courageously resisted the priests of Baal, they had shown great courage in the crisis. But after the fire of persecution came a new great danger. In the reaction and letdown the church at Pergamum, like Elijah, fell into the temptation of ease and relaxation, of decadence, and of forgetting the faith that had carried them through their trial.

I ask you to ask yourselves whether this is or is not a word to us in America. When our fathers came to this land, for many it meant coming out of such persecution. Do we continue truly in our fathers' faith?

To the church at Thyatira, there is again a double word. There is encouragement for good works, love, faith, service, and patient endurance. What else of encouragement could God say? And yet at the same breath of the Spirit the distressing ambiguity of the sin of us all is revealed—Thyatira is worshiping idols, new gods made by the people themselves, and Thyatira is falling into the laxness and immorality that always goes with idolatry. Is Thyatira's condition ours? Where in our Western world is not Thyatira? Dare we assume this word is not addressed by God to us?

To Sardis is the most devastating word. In essence, God says, "You look alive but you really are dead. Repent before judgment comes." To whom, and to which churches is this word addressed? Surely this word should make every congregation look to its life, its activities, and its inner spirit.

In contrast, to Philadelphia, a church that in the world's view is so small and weak and is really insignificant—like the Church of South India, lost in the teeming millions of Hindus, Buddhists, and Muslims, as well as secularists—God says, "Behold, I have set before you an open door, which no one is able to shut" (Rev. 3:8b). "You have kept my word. No earthly power can crush you." Let us thank God that he is able to open doors everywhere and keep them open to faithful people.

And finally, the most familiar and the most disturbing word of all, to the church at Laodicea. Lukewarm. Neither hot nor cold, just decent, self-satisfied, complacent, saying, "I am rich," but being actually poor and naked. To whom does God say this terrible word? Pray to him that it may not be to us.

But this cannot be the last word to the churches; it was not John's last word, for God's last word is always one of promise. John pictures Jesus at a door—at our door, at the door of every church that bears his name, at the door of every Christian heart—"Behold, I stand at the door and knock; if any one hears my voice and opens the door, I will come in to him and eat with him, and he with me" (Rev. 3:20). The promise and the reward and the joy are in his presence with us, his fellowship, his communion.

Still it is true. Outside he stands. He knocks. He does not force his way in, even into a church that bears his name. Patiently he waits for our response.

Christianity According to Christ

"You search the scriptures, because you think that in them you have eternal life; and it is they that bear witness to me."   —JOHN 5:39

O WHAT MAKES THE BIBLE of intrinsic value to man? Why do we believe that it transcends and excels all literature of every form and variety? Because it is the revelation of God to man, containing the words of eternal life, the directive for godly living.

"All scripture is inspired by God," wrote the author of the second letter to Timothy, "and profitable for teaching, for reproof, for correction, and for training in righteousness, that the man of God may be complete, equipped for every good work" (2 Tim. 3:16-17). This is what makes the Bible of such transcendent value to man, it is God-inspired, and being of divine origin it speaks with authority that is supreme, an authority which cannot and should not be challenged.

THE MOST REVEREND METROPOLITAN ANTONY BASHIR, Archbishop of the Archdiocese of New York and All North America, Syrian Antiochian Orthodox Church

Anyone who earnestly and prayerfully studies the Holy Book with an open mind cannot help but reach some definite, irrefutable conclusions: the oneness and the unchangeableness of God, and the oneness and the solidarity of the human race. These are the over-all concepts and teachings of the Old and New Testaments; whatever else they teach is to be considered in the light of these facts. There is no higher concept that we men could entertain than the belief that God is the first cause, the Father, who is the fountainhead of all created beings and objects both visible and invisible.

The one-God, one-world idea runs through the Bible from Genesis to Revelation. We say ours is a republic indivisible, so should be our world! A divided world is like a divided house; it cannot endure very long. One of the great prophets of old cried, "Have we not all one father? Has not one God created us? Why then are we faithless to one another?" (Mal. 2:10a)

Jesus, whom we believe to be history's most outstanding figure and teacher, said, "Pray . . . like this: Our Father" (Matt. 6:9a). Even when one prays privately. Paul in Athens on Mars Hill, was no less explicit when he declared that God "made from one every nation of men to live on all the face of the earth" (Acts 17:26a).

In spite of the clear teachings of the Book, we mortal men set up our own will against the will of God, with the result that today we have a decimated, divided world. In Syria and Lebanon, Christians are called by the Muslims *Ahlul Kitab,* that is, the "People of the Book," a recognition that our beliefs are based upon the revelations of the truth contained therein. This is true only in a poetic and academic sense but not in practice with most of us. The kind of Christianity we manifest is a far cry from the one revealed and practiced by the Master, in the sense that these truths remain within the covers of the Book. We believe them to be impractical in so far as we are concerned.

We have cherished areas in our minds where no one may intrude, not even the Master. Trust and obedience are the basic principles upon which an ordered, mature, happy, harmonious life is established. Yet trust and obedience may mean different things to different people. The question arises, Whom should we trust, and to whom do we owe allegiance? Are our thoughts to be governed by the Holy Spirit, or are they to be influenced by a sense of expediency? To the person who has been regenerated, whose heart and mind are indwelt by the Holy Spirit, there is no alternative. God and God alone is the arbiter in the forum of conscience. Religion is a matter of convictions and not convenience and shall never become vocal and vital in any person's life as long as it is one of his secondary interests, as long as he gives it second place in his thinking and living.

When we try to arrive at a satisfactory answer as to what constitutes true religion, we discover that God and man are two inescapable entities. For no one can actually pray to and worship God, no one can think of Christ in a creative, constructive sense, without thinking upon man, and associating the two as life's most supreme realities. When, for instance, we review the moral laws, the Ten Commandments, upon which all laws are predicated, we discover that the first four Commandments concern themselves with one's relationships to God, and the other six have to do with one's relationships to other men. This is highly significant. If we are to have no other gods before the Almighty, if we are not to become idolatrous, if we are not to take the name of the Lord in vain, if we are to remember the sabbath day to keep it holy, then we should carry these principles into the areas of all human relationships—political, social, and financial, into everyday life and practice.

The prophet Micah tells us in a vivid and unmistakable way what practical religion is. It is not in the offerings alone that true religion is manifested, but also in civic righteousness and social justice. "What does the Lord require of you," he cried, "but to do justice, and to love kindness, and to walk humbly with your God?" (Mic. 6:8b)

Jesus' Sermon on the Mount is considered the world's greatest Bill of Rights, the manifesto of the King, and the most inspiring instrument for righteous living. A careful reading of it yields three definite principles: what should be a person's attitude toward God, toward man, and toward one's self. The whole duty of man resolves itself in proper consideration of these three definite attitudes.

What should be a person's attitude to his Maker according to Jesus Christ? It should be one of sincere love and devotion so that in the various aspects of worship God's honor and glory should be the objective. Thanksgiving, prayer, and fasting are to be practiced, not to be seen of men, not for self-interest, but all these activities should be exercised so that we may be found pleasing to the heavenly Father who, though he sees in secret, will reward the faithful ones openly.

Measuring ourselves by these declarations of the Master, we should be ashamed of our behavior. Oftentimes, we seek recognition, the praises and plaudits of men. It seems as though most of us have not as yet learned the rudiments of Christianity.

Come further with me and let us discover what man's attitude should be toward his brother man. According to Jesus, a person's attitude toward others should be one of benevolence, love, and peace. Contempt for human beings is one of the major sins of society; disdain and ridicule for those who are not in our social or intellectual class occasioned serious troubles in the ranks of men throughout history. Men either rise or fall depending upon their attitudes toward others. Before attempting to make an offering one should be reconciled to his brother man, else it will not be accepted.

One of the paradoxes of Christianity is that one should love his enemy. "Love your enemies," said Jesus, "and pray for those who persecute you, so that you may be sons of your Father" (Matt. 5:44b-45a).

What should be a person's attitude toward himself, according to Christ? Jesus asserts that the first rung up the Christian ladder is one of utter denial, of self-expenditure. The flesh must never be in control of the citadel of man's soul, but rather must give way to the spirit. "If any man would come after me," said Jesus, "let him deny himself and take up his cross and follow me" (Matt. 16:24b).

The world is full of people who profess all kinds of creeds, and those creeds are interpreted in some intricate, hard-to-understand theological terms which confuse the lay mind. One of the unfortunate things about the Christian religion is the great difference between the various groups. Each believes that his brand of religion is better than that of the other groups. These religious differences have, from the beginning, created a wall, a barrier between people, thrown them apart, divided them up until there is scarcely any harmony or unity among people who profess belief in Christ.

Christianity today is almost a contradiction of what Christ intended it to be. The one-God, one-faith, one-world concept conceived and proclaimed by Jesus, is too often being lost sight of in this day and time. We, as Christians, need to go back to the basic teachings of Christianity and recapture the simplicity, the beauty, and the profundity of our faith.

The world needs God-loving, man-loving enthusiasts who realize that life is an opportunity to render the greatest service to the greatest number of people. There is no one who has not at some time or other faced himself with questions like these: Is there a purpose in living, and if there is, what is that purpose? What is the chief end of man? According to one of the great definitions, "The chief end of man is to glorify God and enjoy him forever." But one could not enjoy God and glorify him without self-giving, putting one's self at the disposal and the command of God. Self-giving was the secret of Jesus' power in conquering the souls of men and capturing their love and admiration. Jesus was the personification of love and service. He interpreted the heavenly Father's love to humanity in terms of service, in alleviating human suffering by ministering to every need.

The world's wounds are deep and present-day conditions seem to make them worse. But, thank God, we are not without hope. The Christian people, under God, possess the healing remedy for the world's numerous ills. What an opportunity this is for Christian people to exercise their prerogative in manifesting God's love to a strife-torn, war-torn, hate-infested world.

What this world needs is less selfishness and more self-giving, less criticism and more sympathy, less misunderstanding and more consideration, less hate and prejudice and intolerance, and more love, sympathy, and tolerance. The world needs God and needs him desperately. Enthrone God and his principles in your life; and what a difference that will make!

The Most Meaningful Recollection

✝ THE WRITER OF THE 105th Psalm is a man who finds himself by recollecting God's providence over his people. In reviewing history he experiences the fact of being one of the covenanted people of God, and is brought to open his psalm with a joyful invitation:

> O give thanks to the Lord,
> call on his name,
> make known his deeds among the peoples!

The occasion of the tenth anniversary of the National Council of Churches also calls for retrospect. For the history of the Council in this short span of time there is no reason to be proud of ourselves, but there is a fact in that history for which we may praise the Lord, at the same time that we are brought more earnestly to call upon his name.

Like the psalmist we find that he works through us even if he has to work in spite of us: we discover that we are his church. And our praise and prayer combine so to make

DR. ZOLTAN BEKY, Bishop of the Hungarian Reformed Church in America

known his deeds among the people. Unto this end may our ministry of God's Word be to our own church and to all the churches in and outside the National Council. The recollection of the past, we believe, should inspire us to a grateful recognition of God's covenant with us and a prayerful seeking to realize the gospel which has come to us by making known his deeds among the people.

In the first place, the Christian cannot recall his past without joining the psalmist in saying, "Give thanks to the Lord. . . . Sing to him, sing praises to him, tell of all his wonderful works!" (Ps. 105:1a, 2) This biblical thanksgiving has God for its object, he who is the author of the wondrous works among us. Here is a way of living which is from God and unto God.

What will the newspaper reports tell about our anniversary? Will the reporters be moved to bring to the public a spontaneous song of praise because of our recognition of what God has done and is to us? Or will they only elaborate on the growth of our organization and the activities on which we spend our time?

God gives us reason to be grateful for the National Council into which he has brought our churches and in which he is overcoming our sinful and sectarian witness. Indeed there is ground to be thankful for our Council. But it is God who by our organized unity, and in spite of ourselves, is leading us to experience the joy of being one in Jesus Christ our Lord. Those who have gone before us labored to bring the denominations together and constitute the Federal Council of the Churches of Christ by emphasizing the practical need for Christian unity and outreach.

The historian of the Federal Council has pointed out how it steered away from theological justification, while "the line between organic unity and practical cooperation was carefully drawn, the former being disclaimed as fervently as the latter was extolled." I dare say we have come to see the impossibility of such a distinction. What was to be first a functional approach and organization is coming to be a judgment on denominationalism and provincialism in our American Protestantism, a fact we as a Hungarian Reformed Church in America did not always take seriously. But what has been said with regard to the World Council of Churches, we feel justified to apply to the National Council, namely, that in this body we "have a foretaste of the unity of God's people."

God has led us to bring crisis upon our self-satisfied and active denominations. And we praise him for the National Council of Churches which challenges the particular churches today to be the church and to find our justification in that fact. Of course, each member church should in turn challenge the right and activities of the National Council of Churches in the light of the *Una Sancta*.

The fact that as churches and as a council of churches we are so often lost in our activities that we cannot stop to cast our view backwards, that we do not take stock, is, I believe, the main reason why we lack the joy and praise which should be ours. We are more in need of prayer, than in need of activity.

Here is another element in the wholeness of our text. Should we not yield to the call of the psalmist:

> Glory in his holy name;
>   let the hearts of those who seek the Lord rejoice!
> Seek the Lord and his strength,
>   seek his presence continually!
>
> —Psalm 105:3-4

Our thanksgiving, if true, will always be in the sense of a lack of strength and a call to God. How strong we "feel" we are, and how often our assemblies are taken up by our own activities! I met a delegate to the Presbyterian World Alliance meeting in Brazil in 1959. He was simply worn out and told me that he would have to "get over" the assembly. Incidentally, he referred to an attendant of that assembly, and not a Presbyterian, who time and again felt the need to ask if the leading of the Holy Spirit was sought in the course of the discussions. It was Karl Barth who in the twenties, and often afterward, criticized the self-assurance of our churches and the ecumenical movements.

And here again, I am sure, if we take time to recollect the course of our activities, we will soon be ashamed. Maybe the reason why we all are so unwilling to stop and take stock, is because we do not want to be discouraged. Does Paul warn us in vain, saying, "Therefore let any one who thinks that he stands take heed lest he fall" (1 Cor. 10:12)? When this busy man of God ran the risk of self-exaltation, God said to him, "My grace is sufficient for you, for my power is made perfect in weakness," and the apostle affirms, "I will all the more gladly boast of my weaknesses, that the power of Christ may rest upon me" (2 Cor. 12:9b). Should we not start from this angle again? Should we not relate these biblical truths to our Council, our churches, and ourselves?

If we would cast our eyes backward, see ourselves in the mirror of time, the joyful experience of God's grasp on us and the giving away of our own self-confidence could make us so much better witnesses for him among the people. Then we would heed the voice of the poet:

> Remember the wonderful works that he has done,
>   his miracles, and the judgments he uttered.
>   —Psalm 105:5

To start from this point is to affirm the thesis on *witness* which a preparatory paper on the theme of the 1961 World Council of Churches assembly puts as follows: "God is his

own witness. Wherever the Holy Spirit moves there is witness. The church is created to be God's witness in the world.
It is the fellowship of the Spirit through which men share
in the ongoing action of God."

This source so well defines what it is to make God's deeds
known among the people, that it is worthwhile to quote
from it again: "It is God's plan that his light shall penetrate
to the end of the earth. It is only because it is meant for the
whole world that the light has come to us. If we use and
enjoy it for ourselves alone we stand in the way of God's
plan."

This is our Christian vocation: to make known his deeds
among the people. Personal in nature, our churches and the
National Council of Churches are called upon to extend our
witness. Let us not be confident in the means we have ac-
quired, or the "prestige" our movement has obtained, to get
our witness through to the outside world. Rather, let us rejoice in the recollection of what God has done for us. And
may the thanks and the prayers of the National Council of
Churches and its witness always center in the fact that

> He is the Lord our God;
>   his judgments are in all the earth.
> He is mindful of his covenant for ever,
>   of the word that he commanded, for a
>   thousand generations.
>   —Psalm 105:7-8

We know that what we want the National Council of
Churches to be is the responsibility of each of its constituent
members. With thanks and prayers in behalf of our denomination we pledge again to you, our brethren in Jesus Christ,
as I did in my acceptance speech:

We wish to assure you that with all our abilities and efforts we will fully cooperate with you and do everything within our power to promote your great ecumenical aims, help to achieve a larger and deeper oneness—in faith and doctrine—of all the Christian churches throughout the world.

The Jericho Road
Across Our World

✝ THE JERICHO ROAD twisted dangerously from Jerusalem
downward through Jericho into the Jordan River Valley. It had been a hard road to build and it was a hard road
to maintain. On one side of the road the precipices climbed
sharply upward and on the other side there were yawning
abysses. Both above and below the road there were caves and
crevasses where thieves and marauders could lie in wait.

One day a certain lawyer came to the Master as he stood
at the top of this road, and asked, "What shall I do that I
might have this eternal life of which you speak so frequently?" Jesus, in easy questioning, got him to set forth his own
analysis of the law. The lawyer made a good summary. "The
law," he said, "focuses chiefly upon love; love for God and
love for neighbor."

This set the stage for Jesus to etch in sharp and dramatic
focus an incomparable picture. It was for the lawyer, but it
was also for all men of all time. He said, in essence, "If you
would understand the meaning of the law, if you would have

DR. DESMOND W. BITTINGER, Minister, the Church of the
Brethren; President of McPherson College, McPherson, Kansas

rich and eternal life, give attention to this Jericho road." Then he peopled the Jericho road.

This Jericho road still stretches in the same crooked manner across our world. It runs through every community, twists across every mountain, winds through every valley, touches every city. It can be walked upon in New York and in Moscow, in Hong Kong and Chicago, in Tokyo and Rangoon, in Calcutta and in Berlin. If we would understand, in our day, this rich and eternal life, which can begin now and achieve continuing enrichment, we also should stand near the Lord and give consideration to the Jericho road.

The first person to come to attention on the Jericho road that Jesus described was the sufferer. He lay unattended and forgotten in his suffering.

On the Jericho roads of our day this sufferer still lies; he is often unattended. Any Christian who has the love of Christ in him, or seeks to attain it, cannot bypass the sufferer. Bypassing the sufferer callouses the one who does the bypassing; it eventually destroys within him the compassion which leads to richness of life and to eternal life.

The sufferers on this long road have been and still are many. Recently, a small group of us were in one of the larger refugee camps in Berlin; it was time for the noonday meal. The food, a rather thick stew, was brought to the refugees in large galvanized pails like those which we use in this country for the collecting of garbage. Such pails were used because they were substantial and were well fitted for that kind of service. From them the soup was ladled out into tin containers held by the refugees. In one room three refugee families were separated from one another only by blankets. The space was so constricted that some members of the family had to sit on the second or even the third deck of beds in their small curtained-off compartment, so that there would be elbowroom to eat.

After we had greeted them at the meal we were taken into a basement room within this former large factory building that now served to house refugees. In the basement we sat around tables and were given the same kind of tin utensils that the refugees used. These were filled from the same pails of soup that we had seen being used for the refugees. The intent was that we, the visitors, should share a meal in brotherhood with the refugees.

Some of the Americans within the group had a little difficulty enjoying this meal. A member of our visiting party, however, a Latin American who had come from the mountains of the Andean Indians of Ecuador, called eagerly for a second helping. He said, in a language which mixed together Spanish, German, and English, "This is very good. None of my people in the high mountains ever have this much food at one time during their whole lives. *Es ist gut.*"

At the same table, a man and his wife from India who worked among the village people, said: "You of America feel sorry that these refugees must be housed three families to a room. In India there are thousands, even millions, who throughout their lifetime never have a room. They sleep on the streets and, finally, when they feel death coming close, they try to beg or earn a few cents with which they can rent space in a room where among other similar people they can die. Millions in India would rejoice at these rooms and this food."

A young man in the company who came from the interior of Africa said, "And in Africa, famine sweeps often across our land and my people die for lack of food. This much food would be manna from heaven for them."

These are some of the places where suffering still exists on the Jericho road. Jesus says, "If you would have rich and eternal life, give consideration to the Jericho road."

The second consideration on the Jericho road focuses on

the churchmen who walked down the road. Jesus told of a priest who was hastening to Jericho and of a Levite who followed him. It may be that they were to conduct synagogue services in Jericho and each was intent upon the role he must fulfill. The priest may have been trying to fasten in his mind the points of his sermon. The Levite, similarly, may have been focusing his attention upon the order of the service. Or their attention may have been upon more mundane matters. In any case they saw the sufferer only dimly, for their concentration was elsewhere. They passed him by.

Across our land church steeples stand high. In every European village they add picturesqueness as they strain toward the sky. Within these churches in Europe and America the order of service is carefully worked out. The litanies are not violated. The worshipers come, observe or participate in the service, and go. But this litany and worship did not keep back the planes that flew above the churches and dropped bombs. Many of the churches crumbled and fell, even upon those who regularly worshiped within them. Could it be that the focus of the church was too much upon the preservation of the institution and the litanies of the church? Was Jesus saying that the importance of the litany and the institution may come easily to stand above the importance of the suffering individual? of any individual?

Is it not true that some of the massive cathedrals of the world were built out of the sweat and blood and toil of serfs? And did not some of these work under religious masters who regularly attended the religious services? Although these cathedrals in our day stand as great and beautiful monuments to the church, do they not also stand as monuments to the suffering of forced and degraded labor in many instances?

A judge in a municipal women's court in Chicago recently undertook to parole to her church a fourth-time woman violator of the law. This woman had four small children in her charge. The woman replied to the judge's suggestion that he parole her to her pastor, "I have no pastor."

The judge inquired, "But surely you know a rabbi, a priest, a Protestant minister?"

Her reply was an indictment of the church. "I have never known a pastor, a rabbi, a priest. I have no church."

Jesus says, "If you would have the life that is rich and eternal, give consideration to the church. It should have many concerns about itself and its relationship to the Jericho road."

A third focus of attention along the Jericho road is implied in Jesus' story. His whole life and teaching emphasized it. It is that the Christian must forever be concerned about the road itself.

Even if the travelers on the road, churchmen and others, spent much of their time and millions of their dollars to relieve the suffering on the road, the suffering would still continue. The concerned must do something to relieve the cause of the suffering. The hiding places of the robbers on the road need to be filled in; the dangerous precipices over which people may fall need to have guardrails; the road needs to be straightened and improved. The church has worked at this through many agencies, but much remains to be done.

Our expenditures for "defense" go beyond forty billion dollars. We are not at war. It is the hope of our government and the governments of the world that war is not imminent, even that war may never again occur on a world-wide scale. Does not the spending of forty billions for defense, contrasted with three and one-half billions for education, sharply indict us? Does it not say much about our interests and our fears?

Let us look at some bumps in the road which need attending:

In spite of our high prosperity we are told that a third of our housing in America continues to be substandard; across the world the average is twice that.

We are beset with strikes, even though the losses to labor and industry cry out that force offers no real way to permanent progress for any segment of a group or for the whole group.

In legislation we spend much time talking. Local interests sometimes overshadow the interest of the whole nation or of the world in these talks; prejudice sometimes overrules justice.

In international affairs fear and mistrust often keep us from having a normal flow of goods and services; mistrust stifles scientific exchange, it muffles international conversations and negotiations.

There are many in our world who are not yet free; free to think as they wish, free to direct their own affairs; not only is there an "ugly American," but there are also other "ugly" people.

This is not to say that all stretches of the Jericho road are bad. Much has been done to improve the road, but there still remain areas where the Jericho road needs to be straightened and improved.

Jesus says, "If you would have eternal life, give consideration to the Jericho road."

A fourth concern along the Jericho road is an extremely important one. It is, for many, the most difficult to achieve. We must love the robber who despoils the road.

The job of the Christian is not done, in fact, it is not even begun until his love "searches" for the despoiler of the road, the lost and wicked one, and seeks to bring him to reclamation and redemption. This points quite an opposite direction from that which our personal and national policies have often followed. Instead of speaking of redemption for those who endanger the national community, each nation has spent vast sums in order to destroy the "robber," and to destroy the robber's nation. Each nation always reserves for itself the right to identify who the robber is and to take appropriate punitive action. Thus, we each usually place the other in the role of the robber and set out to destroy rather than to help this enemy.

The love and concern of our Savior encompassed those who hanged him upon the cross; it was big enough to include the thief who hung with him and all who stood round about. It included his mother; it included John; but it included, also, the "enemy."

One of the most difficult parts of our journey as we travel the Jericho road is to be concerned redemptively for the despoilers of the road. They must be redeemed as individuals and reclaimed as groups. When Jesus says, "If you would have eternal life, give consideration to the Jericho road," his love includes also the robber.

This is a sharp, clear admonition to the church and to Christians of our day: Walk forward on the Jericho roads which twist perpetually through our world and our times, help the sufferer, deepen and broaden the sensitivity and involvement of the church in every facet of mankind's daily life, improve the road itself, and seek forever to bring to redemption the despoiler of the road.

Stand Still in the Light

☩ "STAND STILL." These words recur like a refrain in a brief epistle of George Fox written in 1652. Friends are told to "stand still in trouble and see the strength of the Lord," to "stand still in that which is pure after ye see yourselves," to "stand still in the Light that shows them . . . temptations, corruptions, uncleanness," to "stand still in that Power which brings peace," and, with the same meaning, to "sink down in that which is pure, and all will be hushed and fly away."

The date of this letter is significant. In 1652 the Quaker movement received its first great impetus and gained thousands of adherents. Friends have probably never been more active and uplifted than they were in that first great year, when it seemed that a new "day of the Lord" was dawning. How then can we explain this quietistic advice to stand still, coming as it did from the most active Quaker of them all? Would it not have been more appropriate if Fox had advised Friends to be busy in the Light?

One answer to this question can be found in the need for inner strength and composure sufficient for meeting and

HOWARD H. BRINTON, member of the Philadelphia Yearly Meeting of the Religious Society of Friends; formerly director of Pendle Hill, Quaker study center

overcoming powerful destructive forces. During the first forty years of Quaker history no effort was spared by church and state to destroy the new movement. But, although Lutherans and the German states had succeeded in crushing the Anabaptists in Germany, Anglicans and Puritans did not succeed in crushing Quakers in England. Perhaps this was partly because Quakers had discovered a form of worship which taught them how to stand still in the Light. In the midst of the struggle and suffering they could, either in their meetings or elsewhere, retreat to a "quiet habitation within," a place where "all will be hushed and fly away."

Such a retreat did not necessarily mean a withdrawal from activity, as is shown by other figures of speech used by Fox to express similar advice. Friends are told to "stand faithful to the Lord God and his Power and Truth, that their heads may not sink in the storms but may be kept above the waves." "Do not," he says elsewhere, "gad about from the Truth Within, that ye may be kept above all high-swelling storms, bustlings, and tempests and with it ye may be kept over the world." This does not mean that Friends should flee from the storm but rather that, although their bodies are in it, their heads should be above it in the calm and serene presence of the Light.

There were other reasons for standing still in the Light, for in 1652 persecution, though it had begun, was far from having reached the intensity of ten years later. Light, including divine light, is that which reveals. "Stand still," says Fox, "in that which shows and discovers." Clearly it discovers our own sins and weaknesses, for we are asked to "stand still after we see ourselves." Self-examination in the Light must come first—in the Light, because the Light reveals obstacles which stand between it and ourselves. Their dark shadows must be removed before we can see clearly. The medieval mystics likewise declared that purgation is the necessary first stage in spiritual progress on the way to the second stage, which is illumination.

But the revelation of truth about ourselves is not the only function of the Light, for the light is also moral and religious truth in a broader sense. Here we must understand the meaning of that essentially quietistic word pure. When we seek in Fox's words to stand still in that which is pure, we try to find a truth which is purified because it is not contaminated by our own prejudices and preconceptions. The truth is pure and above the world because it is free from the worldly conventional opinions of society around us.

By seeking and sometimes finding that which is purified of conventionalities, Friends became a nonconformist minority in the midst of a hostile majority. In dress, speech, and behavior they were not afraid to be different though not, at least at first, for the sake of being different. They became pioneers in a number of social causes because they had recourse to a source of truth other than the voice of society. The Quaker position in these causes has now become generally accepted by the "world" with the exception of nonparticipation in war. Since Friends still hold this doctrine, at least officially, they remain a nonconformist minority.

As members of a minority which may again be persecuted for unconventional opinions, they need to learn how to acquire inner strength and peace and to be enabled to "sink down in that which is pure" so that "all will be hushed and fly away." They need also sometimes to quit their bustling and "stand still in the Light" if they are to continue to make new discoveries by facing the truth freshly and directly. This truth is not only found within the New Testament but also without, for the voice of the Christ within must be clarified and interpreted by the words of the Christ of history.

In his letters George Fox is continually advising Friends not to use violence on their troubles or even on their disorderly thoughts by fighting them on their own level but rather to get "atop" of them. "Friends," he says, "take heed of being hurried with many thoughts but live in that which goes over them all." And in 1670, when persecution was waxing especially hot, he writes, "So let your minds and souls and hearts be kept above all outward and visible things."

This, like "standing still in the Light," might seem to many activists a form of escapism. Instead of standing still or "getting over" troubles, should we not endeavor to share the burden of the world's sin and suffering? Did not Fox himself suffer eight imprisonments when he might have avoided them by doing what most other people did? He certainly did not "get over" his suffering by ignoring it as unreal or unimportant. But, paradoxically, he both endured it and rose above it.

Each year the church commemorates the crucifixion and ascension of Christ. At the crucifixion we think of Christ as taking upon himself the burden of the world's sin and suffering. But in the ascension he rose above it to a higher, serener world. He was both in the world and above it, and the inward light, the Christ-spirit in man, is also both in the world and above it. If it be true, as Paul says, that we must be crucified with Christ if we are to rise above the world with him, then we, through his spirit, may also both share the burden of the world's suffering and rise above it.

God's
Greatest Creation

O THIS IS A MARVELOUS WORLD in which we live. A few generations ago, man thought he knew nearly all there was to know, and even then he was aware that he was a citizen in a great universe. Today, we realize that the knowledge of our forefathers was very partial. They would not recognize this world as the same place they knew were they able to return today.

We are finding out so much more of interest about this world of ours, but we are also discovering that there is much we do not know. We wonder what secrets lie locked from us and when they may be revealed. We have become aware today that no man can hope to have complete knowledge of the world. A certain general knowledge is essential to each of us, but we must leave the specialized knowledge to those who devote their lifetime to particular fields. No man's life is long enough and no man's mind is large enough to understand it all.

With all the knowledge that is ours we cannot doubt the

THE REVEREND EARL CRUZAN, Minister of Pawcatuck Seventh Day Baptist Church, Westerly, Rhode Island; member of the Board of Managers of the Seventh Day Baptist Missionary Society and chairman of its Home Field Committee

existence of God. Some will contest this statement. Yet the potentials of the earth and her elements have lain before men for countless years, and our generation has just discovered some of them. Many of these potentials even the generation just before us would have declared impossible. We recognize an order in the universe. The life of the universe and the elements thereof could not just happen. There is too much balance in the realm of nature—one type of life depending upon another, with a certain balance of gases and minerals necessary for life to continue—for this universe to have just happened. It is not a haphazard thing which has come by chance, by trial and error. The very error of such trials would have destroyed life before it began. There is a definite plan that underlies it all.

There is evidence of God, of him who could think and will and act. He could and does think and act in such a way that we are just discovering many of the possibilities of the universe that he has entrusted to us.

If we believe in God, we also believe that man is God's greatest creation. Man is able to think and will and act. Man does not have to depend upon instinct to preserve life and to make it better. Man relies upon the knowledge of the past; he learns from the mistakes of another generation and he profits from the truth that has been learned. It is not necessary that each person discover it for himself. A person meets a situation, appraises it, and decides upon the appropriate action and seeks to carry it through. His decisions are made upon the background of knowledge that is his. Not always does he decide wisely, but more often than not he does.

Each man works independently; yet each works with others. Men are dependent upon one another to know a full life. Contrasted with man is the industry of the bees and the ants—two truly communistic communities among the insects who work only for the common good of the colony with no hope for the individual. Even the queen is so carefully guarded that her life is only to give life to the colony. She has no rule or authority over it.

That which we know, that which we do, God knows in more detail than we know and he is able to do more expertly than we. What is man's relationship to God? From the Scriptures, we discover that man was the last of God's creation. Man came upon this earth by the express desire of God to create a creature in his own image and likeness. Created in the likeness and image of God, man was given the dominion of this universe. And it is largely man's decision as to what he will do with it. Man was created in potential sonship to God. Yet man was given the freedom of choice. Each person is free to stand or to fall by the choices that he makes.

Man standing by himself looks upon his knowledge and his accomplishments with pride. He is still tempted as was Adam to be like unto God—to have the knowledge and power of God. Man says in effect: "Look at me, I am God. I have all knowledge and all power. Look what I can do. I can fly as a bird with supersonic speed. I can swim as the fish even to the depths of the ocean and now even under the icecaps to the North Pole. I traverse the earth quickly. I am not limited by time and space. I have conquered it as I have put the elements of the earth to work for myself."

Each man standing by himself is in conflict with another man standing by himself. Except as men learn to work together, no man can go very far. Working together with each doing a part, we can accomplish much. Yet each has to observe certain rules and regulations. As an individual, man is definitely limited. Each has to admit: "I don't know it all." He must also admit that God does know it all. He must recognize that in God rests all knowledge and power.

Sin comes into the life of man. Sin is man himself as God.

Man standing in his own strength and his own knowledge is sin—man saying: "I am the most important; I want what will give me satisfaction; if that treads upon somebody else's toes, I still want it, and if I can, I'll get it, for that is important."

Man stands first of all in a created relationship to God. Created in his image and after his likeness he is capable of sonship and fellowship with him.

Man takes upon himself an assumed relationship. He does this by assuming that he is as God, that he knows it all, that he is all-important, that his desires are the only reality in life. Men alienate themselves from God through their sin. This is their assumed relationship. It brings only pain and sorrow. And after a while it brings a sense of futility. Man has to keep busy in this role he has set for himself or his life becomes stale and he wonders what the trouble may be.

There is also for man the possibility of a restored relationship. Potentially, every man is a redeemed soul even as he is a created soul. He may not be redeemed because he refuses to accept the price of his redemption. Yet it is offered to him.

Man's choices often take him away from God; they often take him deep into the mire of sin, but his worth is greater than his choices. Jesus' parable of the prodigal son illustrates man's worth. The son could have lived with his father, yet he was not forced to remain. He demanded his right; he went his own way. He lived in sin and squandered his birthright. When he came to himself, he was about as low as a man could go. He returned home a humbled soul and was received and restored to sonship. He was received according to the potential that had been his in the beginning.

This is each one's possibility with God. There is a restored relationship for each one who will accept it. To do so one must recognize his sin. Even as Alcoholics Anonymous

cannot help an alcoholic until he recognizes that he is hope-
lessly an alcoholic and cannot restore himself, even so each
one must recognize his sin. Man must realize that of himself
he cannot raise himself to the level of God. It takes humility
to admit that one is a sinner; even as it takes humility to
admit that one is a wretched bondslave to drink. Once one
has admitted it, the first step is taken and the way is open
before him.

There is forgiveness for such a man. God is ready to give
it freely. Man may renounce God and his teachings, yet he
remains God's greatest creation. God is ready to restore him
to his proper relationship whenever man is ready for it.
Christ has paid the penalty for each man's sins. If a man believes that God loves him, that he needs forgiveness, and if
he seeks to follow in God's way, forgiveness is his.

This is a busy age. There is so much that man wants to do
that he cannot do it all. He goes around in a frenzy almost
as though he feared missing something of life. The reality
of living takes time. It is not found in the continual press
of activity.

Living that is real takes into account everything about us;
especially *everybody* about us. Man is often so busy living
that he does not realize that while the days are slipping by
his character is being formed. He does not realize that bit by
bit the habits of life are molding him, that the respect of
friends and neighbors is being earned or forfeited. What man
hopes to do and expects to be cannot be accomplished overnight. He has to work toward it. He cannot arrive at a certain place in this world's struggle to get ahead, to gain material goods at the expense of others, and then suddenly
change and become considerate and friendly, a good neighbor respected for his integrity. The motivation of his life
must be changed. He cannot deliberately set his goal in one
direction, expecting that after a period of years he can as

easily set it in another. But he can change if he lets Christ come into his life.

Many people have changed, but man does not do it by calculating to lead one kind of life for twenty or thirty years and then to lead another kind the rest of his life. But if he will let Christ come into his life he can change even as did Zacchaeus. Zacchaeus was a grasping tax collector, wealthy and despised. When Christ came into his life, he changed. He gave back that which he had taken unfairly; yet I can imagine that it was a long time before his acquaintances ever thought of him as anything but a grasping tax collector.

One must work at it if he is to know God and the fullness of life that is in him. Jesus told of the ten virgins who waited for the coming of the bridegroom. Five of them had oil when the bridegroom came and five were without oil. The five who were prepared entered the house of the festivities. The other five could not get in. Was not Jesus saying that one cannot get ready in a hurry?

Yes, man is God's greatest creation. He was created for potential sonship and fellowship with God. Yet he is given the freedom of choice. Man often chooses evil and sin. Even then, before God man is worth more than the result of his choices. He is worth enough to be redeemed as a son if he will recognize his need for forgiveness and claim the sacrifice of Christ for himself.

God has not left his greatest creation, man, to destroy himself. He has given him freedom to go his own way, yet he has offered him pardon and restoration if he will accept it. Once man has accepted forgiveness, God would have him build into his life those things which endure for eternity. Man's worth is greater than the result of his choices. Even when his choices have taken him deep into degradation and sin, if he will look to God, God will restore him to sonship.

The One Thing We Need

> "For truly, I say to you, if you have faith as a grain of mustard seed, you will say to this mountain, 'Move hence to yonder place,' and it will move; and nothing will be impossible to you."
> —MATTHEW 17:20b

THERE IS SOMETHING in life without which we cannot live. Without it we cannot plan for the future, nor deal with our fellow men in confidence, nor look forward in hope, nor efficiently use the energies of body and mind. Without it, worry haunts the mind, skepticism invades the outlook, and disillusionment warps experience. With complete lack of it, a man would not expect the sunrise tomorrow, would not dare to engage in business, would not be sure of his family's love, would build no school or church or city. In short, life would be impossible without this one essential—faith. Faith is the motive power of living and the warp and woof woven into all the pattern of life.

Reading the Gospels one finds a surprising emphasis on believing. Jesus went up and down the land urging men to have faith. That summons runs like a refrain through almost

DR. MARION DE VELDER, Minister of Central Reformed Church, Grand Rapids, Michigan; President of the Board of Education of the Reformed Church in America

every conversation and incident. He was filled with joy and gratitude whenever he came upon people who believed. He healed the bodies and forgave the sins of those who had faith. Listen to his words: "Go your way; your faith has made you well" (Mark 10:52b). . . . "According to your faith be it done to you" (Matt. 9:29b). . . . "Believe in God, believe also in me" (John 14:1b). . . . "If you have faith . . . nothing will be impossible to you" (Matt. 17:20b).

Ultimately we must have faith in something or someone, or life comes to a standstill and finally breaks down. Faith alone can save men for it *looks beyond the horizon*. It strikes out boldly into the unknown, and ventures beyond the knowledge we have or the things we see. It goes beyond science, for science records the observation and discoveries of men in relation to the physical universe. Faith lives through and beyond history, for history records the past life of men in relation to one another. Science without faith would be merely blind experiment and history without faith would be an endless collection of human doing on a dead level without a glimmer of hope. Faith alone keeps the laboratory investigator persistently pursuing his quest for new facts, and it holds the hope for the future because it keeps men of vision fearlessly applying ideals to present conditions and issues.

Faith is the pioneering, adventuring quality that opens up new areas of life and thought. It is the mainspring of effort in untried projects. Faith sent the Wright brothers into the air, Columbus on his westward voyage, Pasteur to studying germs, and Graham Taylor into the Chicago slums. Faith in God called Abraham into a strange country, Isaiah to minister to a people of unclean lips, Jesus to the cross, and Paul into the Gentile world. Religion is impossible without faith, for it undergirds life with courage, patience, and meaning and brings a man into direct communion with God.

Broadly speaking, faith is either holding for true something which is not already verified in experience or demonstrated by logical conclusion, or confidence in the integrity of a person. In the first instance it means "believe" and in the second it means "trust." An example of the first would be the belief in the persistence of personality after death, and of the second the "plighting" of the troth in the marriage ceremony.

Faith is not blind credulity, as one small boy defined faith as "believing things you know ain't so!" Real faith is believing things because you know they must be so. Augustine said, "Faith is to believe what we do not see and the reward of this faith is to see what we believe."

Faith may be described under three categories: choice, acceptance, and action. First is *choice*—or choosing whom we will serve. The trouble with the well-meant and all too common practice of urging people to have more faith is that the injunction misses the real point. Everybody has some faith. It is not a question of faith or no faith. The amount of faith in circulation seems to be quite abundant—one wonders at times, seeing the way faith is misapplied, whether there is not too much! But that is not the issue. The main question is: What is the object of our faith? In what or in whom do we put our trust? In what do we really believe and by what do we live? Shall it be in ourselves, in our friends, in our loved ones, in "humanity," in some economic or political arrangement, in democracy or totalitarianism? or shall it be faith in God, and if so, what kind of God?

Much of the tragedy and difficulty in our world can be explained on the basis of misdirected faith. The pity is that we trust so many things which are not worthy of our highest devotion. When our faith is on the human level only, trouble dogs us. Jesus sensed this with penetrating insight when he said, "No one can serve two masters; for either he will hate the one and love the other, or he will be devoted to the one and despise the other. You cannot serve God and mammon" (Matt. 6:24). There you have the searching analysis: Men cannot have faith in these two at the same time. First, then, Christian faith is making the right choice for our devotion.

The second is *acceptance,* accepting things as they are and life as it is. This means the uncomplaining acceptance of the limitations of life. There are some factors in life that cannot be altered. For example, Jesus said, "Which of you by being anxious can add one cubit to his span of life?" (Matt. 6:27) Height, color of eyes, the weather, the limits of physical and mental energy, the need of food and air and sleep, are some of the things given. To fret continually about some unalterable factors of life is a lack of faith. To know our own limitations and weaknesses and yet to go on courageously is to act on faith. To know the idiosyncrasies and foibles of another person and yet to love him is faith. To sense and recognize the limits and checks that God places on human life and then to thrill with the joy of living is glorious faith.

To take life as it is—with all its cruelty, hatred, jealousy, gossip, pettiness—and then to do what we can to make it better and nobler, is to demonstrate faith. To look upon our present world with all its stupidity, its crass selfishness, its prodigal waste, its callous disregard for human life, and to refuse to give up hope but to see it all clearly, to purify our own hearts and join hands with others to love and not to hate, to work confidently under God's guidance and in his power, and to believe that truth will triumph—this is faith which knows no defeat. Josiah Royce defined faith as "the soul's insight, or discovery of some reality, that will enable a man to stand anything that may happen to him in the universe."

Christian faith is the acceptance of life as it is, plus a *forward look*. If faith were mere acceptance it would be little better than cowardice. But it includes a recognition of God's power to change things by working through men. It insists that you must start with a person where he is and as he is if you are to help him go forward. Tertullian defined faith as "patience with its lamp lit," which stresses intelligent waiting coupled with confidence in the power of God to help. In this same mood is the prayer for "good judgment" credited to Reinhold Niebuhr: "O God, give us serenity to accept what cannot be changed; courage to change what can be changed; and the wisdom to know one from the other."

The third quality of faith is found in *action*. The exercise of faith gives us the insight that some things can be altered, which without faith would seem entirely impossible. Such an insight lights up the phrase "faith to remove mountains." It means to believe in all situations and conditions that *God is almighty*. When, as the Gospel record tells us, the disciples saw the man born blind they did not consider the possibility that he might be made to see. They wanted to engage in a discussion on the origin and responsibility of sin, asking, "Who sinned, this man or his parents?" (John 9:2b) Jesus refused to be drawn into this useless discussion and proceeded to heal the man, so that the man himself might see, and that the disciples might be instructed in the meaning of faith and in the use of power to glorify God himself.

Faith means action. It does not sit still in the face of obstacles, but realizes that God has unlimited power, which is available to work in and through those who trust, to do otherwise impossible things. Rudolf K. Bultman has described faith, in the teachings of Jesus, as the strength in concrete situations of life to be serious with a conviction that God is almighty. Faith is taking life as it is and God at his word and then doing something. It is believing farther than you can see and trusting deeper than you can understand, and is venturing to live according to these convictions which can be verified only by trying them at personal risk.

In his book *Marching On,* James Boyd describes the events of the Civil War and gives us an illustration which is close to the kind of faith presented in the New Testament. One of the characters, a Confederate soldier called Ance, after seeing General Robert E. Lee at Gettysburg, says: "He wasn't an extra big man or anything; just what you would call a medium-sized old gentleman and everything about him mighty neat, just so. He was so polite and grave the way he took off his hat to us . . . when I saw him I just naturally knew that whatever he said to do, I would do it. And that it would be the right thing to do too. Yes, Suh." There are two main elements in his attitude: first, whatever was commanded he would do it, obedience; and second, he would be sure that it was right, loyalty and confidence. This attitude is one of simple and complete faith.

Faith is the choice of the right master in life, the loyalty of the whole self to God as revealed in Jesus Christ. It includes acceptance of life as it is, the recognition of our limitations plus the conviction that God is all-powerful. To move forward in this adventurous spirit makes it possible to do the otherwise impossible. Faith is the right relation of a man toward his God, so that God is permitted to do in us and through us that which is greater than we can ask or think.

A person may know all about the technique and the strokes of swimming. He may understand the principles of buoyancy. But he will never learn to swim unless he gets into the water and learns to apply the principles upon which movement in the water depends. So we strike out boldly in the venture of faith. There is no hope for those who will not believe or trust. Those who insist that things are not possible will never learn the thrill of walking by faith. They close the doors upon themselves, and God is not allowed to work through them.

When Jesus came to his home town, it is written, "He did not do many mighty works there, because of their unbelief" (Matt. 13:58). Christ waits to come to us, standing at the door of our generation with abundant power to recreate us and our age, to make it meaningful with divine purpose. But he must have persons who believe in him and through whom he can work out his purposes. He needs people who trust wholeheartedly in him and look to him, like the Confederate soldier, and naturally know that whatever he says to do, do it, and be sure that it is the right thing to do.

The faith that Jesus himself had, produced the most beautiful and victorious life the world has ever seen. We, too, can share in such a life when we venture forth in that faith. Life will take on new meaning and expectancy. We will discover that we actually are "specialists in the impossible." We can stand with the countless faithful of all generations who have put their trust in him and have never been put to shame.

Our world waits for those who have such transforming faith. *You* can be one of that great company who understand and use the faith without which we cannot live. Our Master looks for the venturesome to follow him, but only those who are willing to walk by faith need apply.

Interruptions

While he was thus speaking to them, behold, a ruler came in and knelt before him, saying, "My daughter has just died; but come and lay your hand on her, and she will live." And Jesus rose and followed him, with his disciples. And behold, a woman who had suffered from a hemorrhage for twelve years came up behind him and touched the fringe of his garment. —MATTHEW 9:18-20

☩ HOW OFTEN WE COMPLAIN about being interrupted! And in the main, how right we are! I suppose, if we were required to choose only one word to describe the wild confusion in which this generation has lived, "interruptions" is what it would be—irritatingly, wearyingly everywhere. Everyone of us likes to flatter himself that he is steering his own course, governing his own life. But before any of us knows it, along comes a major cataclysm or a private call to break in on personal plans, to force one to serve someone else's convenience or benefit—and we are tempted to pity ourselves.

The bracing thought with which I want to refresh you

DR. FRANKLIN CLARK FRY, President of The United Lutheran Church in America; President of the Lutheran World Federation; chairman of the executive and central committees of the World Council of Churches

today is: Did you ever think of Jesus? If you will only do so, it will give you an altogether changed slant. Surprising and even jarring as it may sound, the truth is that our Lord was the most interrupted person who ever lived. Looking at him does many wholesome things for us. One of them is that it should surely make us calmer. As we reflect reverently upon him, we will find ourselves becoming less resentful and annoyed.

Does it come as a shock to hear me assert that Jesus was the most interrupted person who ever lived? Well, see for yourself. It was vividly, almost disturbingly, true. The marvel about him was that he remained so divinely serene through it all. *There* is a healthy lesson for us who believe in him as the Son of God.

Look at this incident involving Jairus. When you examine it closely through a spiritual microscope, all it was, was really *two* interruptions. The way Jesus greeted them is the marvel. It ought to be a model for every feverish soul.

When we met Christ in the opening verse of our text, he was teaching. You can be sure that it was nothing trivial! Words of wisdom were flowing from his mouth like pearls of great price, shining and precious. He was in the midst of life-giving instruction. Who knows, it might have ranked with the Sermon on the Mount. Yet right in the heart of it (think how rude it was!) without even a "pardon me," in burst a dignitary of the synagogue. Such poignant distress sobbed in his voice that his plea not only deflected the teaching of Jesus, but what happened was more violent even than that. Jairus *ended* it—for that day at least.

Ponder this terrible thought: Many people must have been present who would never see the Master in the flesh again, for whom his words of truth would remain permanently stunted and dangling because Jairus had broken in. Yet Jesus turned aside at once!

That was interruption number one. As if that were not enough, a second almost tumbled over its heels. If the Lord had been like us, it would have been enough to make him seethe in frustration. In an instant, as the crowd which had been listening placidly began to boil ahead into an excited procession and every heart and muscle was intent only to hurry to the afflicted home, suddenly there came a second distraction, quite as unprovoked. This time a trembling hand was thrust out from the throng. A woman who was diseased and ashamed furtively stretched out her finger tips and barely touched the hem of his garment.

Certainly nothing could have the right to delay the healer now. Nothing should detain him from a dying child. But once again, he pauses. The deep, wonderful, everlasting truth is that when a hand of need is stretched out to anyone else, it may seem like an interruption. To Jesus it was always the touch of God.

What fascinates me further is that these two interruptions are little more than random cuttings out of Jesus' entire life. They are simply tiny instances of what happened to him every day and almost every hour. In all history, has there ever been anyone who was so much the slave of interruptions? Gloriously, not their slave, but their master!

Recall with me another night very early in Jesus' ministry when another ruler, Nicodemus, intruded on his rest. If he had not, we would never have heard: "For God so loved the world that he gave his only Son" (John 3:16a).

Think of the day when Jesus had attracted a congregation around him in the house of a friend. People crowded so close and filled the room so full that no one else could squeeze in. The matchless Savior was feeding souls lavishly then, too, when suddenly the roof opened up and a paralyzed man was let down. That abrupt act punctuated one of

Jesus' priceless sentences right in its middle; yet to this day mankind thrills to the words, "Man, your sins are forgiven you" (Luke 5:20b).

The feeding of the five thousand was an equally exasperating interruption which robbed the Master of well-earned quiet in the country. Even in the Garden of Gethsemane Jesus delayed the solemn act of his arrest by restoring something as trivial as an ear that was cut off. In the upper room, he postponed the very institution of the Holy Communion to wash his disciples' feet. On the cross, even there, we see him putting aside his anguish to pray forgiveness for those who nailed his hands, to comfort a repentant robber, and to provide for his forlorn mother who watched him die.

Actually, the whole of the earthly life of Jesus taken together was the hugest interruption of all time. It was all one great, deeply shadowed break in the glory which he had with the Father before the world was, from which he descended when he was born, and to which he returned only after he had risen to the skies.

There is a new, transfiguring light that needs to be shed into our minds and hearts too. Disappointments, is that what we are tempted to call *our* interruptions? God give us the grace instead to change the "d" to a capital "h" to see them for what they really are—"His appointments."

Three simple guiding ideas are worth keeping in mind. Every time you are tempted to be exasperated, repeat them to yourself and they will help to steady you. The first is this: The very frequency and extent of your interruptions, like Christ's, may well be the measure of the valuableness of your life. Reflect for an instant. His days would never have been so twisted away from the neat patterns that he had planned for them if he had not possessed such sympathy and magnetism. No more will ours be. Only people who are full of help and strength are bombarded with other men's needs. At their highest, the interruptions which we chafe at are the credentials of how indispensible we are. As surely as you brim with usefulness, that is when they will cut in. The greatest condemnation that anyone can incur, the supreme danger to beware of, is to be let comfortably alone.

I know an old lady, God bless her, who is a glowing example that interruptions are a tribute. You would think that she was living in an eddy clean off of the stream of life, but no sooner does she settle herself in her cozy apartment for a quiet week or month than invariably a call comes to minister to another, to care for some invalid, or to give joy to the bereaved, or even to be a happy companion of the young. (There are plenty of old ladies in the same apartment house who are never disturbed.) The demands on her are a deserved compliment to her spirit.

The second reminder is no less searching and stirring—at least to me. It is this: All of this gush of interruptions, from the volcanic ones to the merely nagging ones, only proves, when all is said and done, that you are a *man*. Suppose someone were to ask you what the distinguishing mark of a human being is, what would you say? I know the answer that the biologists would give. Speaking only of the body of man, they would point unhesitatingly to its adaptability. Sobering and humiliating as it is, there is just nothing else in which our physical powers excel the lower animals. Run over the catalogue and you will hang your head. Men do not compare with the elephant in strength, nor with the greyhound in speed. Insects outjump us and fish outswim us. When it comes only to bare living, just stretching out a monotonous existence, the alligator is clean out of our class; it can survive without a thought or a deed of kindness for five hundred years!

Yes, flexibility and adaptability are the distinctive excellence of man; ability to live in the tropics or at the poles, beneath the sea or high in the air, deep down or on a mountain summit. So, just as emphatically, it ought to be with our spirits. My friends, there is nothing sadder nor more to be guarded against than arthritis of personality. We just do not dare to become frozen in the joints of our emotions any more than of our hands. Whenever a man instinctively becomes provoked at every break in his routine, he has begun to slip. Once we start to react as if the schedule is sacred instead of the new duty, it is a sign of senility at any age; it is a proof that we are growing fossilized. And remember, things become fossils only after they are dead! This is another sound, striking reason to thank God for interruptions. They keep a spring in the soul.

Yet the greatest blessing of all that we get from our annoying and sometimes bruising interruptions is the third: They teach reliance on God. More than that, they are apt to compel it! Reluctant as we often are to admit it, the reason why you and I like to organize our lives so snugly and show signs of becoming irritated when any crack appears in our routine does not do great credit to ourselves. It is because we like to delude ourselves that *we* are the masters of our own fate. We flatter ourselves that we can handle whatever comes. We are constantly trying to bring life down into a compass that we can manage.

That, more than anything else, is why we react as we do against any sudden change. It disrupts our complacency. It makes us shaky and timid. It threatens to carry us out beyond our depth. The shattering truth, my friends, is that that is exactly where we ought to be. That is where we receive the most awesome blessing. There we meet God.

After all, is it not a piece of colossal egotism to think that life must always fit itself into our ways? That would make *us* bigger than life! Is it not stupid to think that the world must accommodate itself to our comfort? We are here not to be comfortable but to do and to grow. Our noblest growth comes when we cast ourselves on the Lord. This is the supreme and final benefit of interruptions.

The next time, Christian, you are tempted to rebel and pout when life breaks in on you, remember Jesus Christ. Thank God for the proof that you are valuable, that he keeps you flexible, that he points you to himself.

A Place of Springs

As they go through the valley of Baca they make it a place
of springs.   —PSALM 84:6a

PERHAPS MANY A TIME you have read the beautiful
Psalm 84 or you have heard it read in church, and
have wondered what the valley of Baca was. Let me try an
imaginative interpretation. We shall have to go back more
than two thousand years to those days when many Jews
were dispersed and exiled from their own land. Those who
remained loyal to the faith of their fathers dreamed of nothing with a deeper longing than at least once in their lifetime to make a pilgrimage to Jerusalem, the city of David
where the temple stood, there to celebrate the Passover
festival, to listen to the sacred songs, to participate in the
worship of Jehovah.

Let us accompany one such little band of pilgrims. They
have come a long way, perhaps hundreds of miles, but the
last hill has been climbed, and there before them in the
gleam of the evening sun lies Jerusalem, the city of their
fathers, so hallowed to them through many sacred memories.
As they stand there with hearts full of gratitude one of them,

---

DR. HERBERT GEZORK, President of the American Baptist
Convention, 1959-1960; President of Andover Newton Theological School

51

who may have been a poet, begins to pray. All his deep joy
in reaching their goal, in finding now fulfilled the hopeful
dream of many years, floods from his heart to his lips as he
whispers, "How lovely is thy dwelling place, O Lord of
hosts!" (Ps. 84:1)

Then he recalls the long journey that lies behind them,
all the dangers that beset the little band—the brutal, ruth-
less highway robbers, the hostile people through whose land
they had to travel; and worst of all the long stretches of
sun-baked desert where the eye could see nothing but sand
and rocks, and here and there a prickly little plant called
Baca from which some of these desert valleys may well have
derived their names. And he recalls how they had trudged
along, the sun mercilessly beating down upon them, their
last drop of water gone, fear in their hearts that they might
never reach their goal but die in the desert as so many others
before them.

But one of them had raised his eyes, and far away on the
horizon he had seen a cluster of palm trees. Was it a mirage,
or was it an oasis? With their last strength they had walked
toward it. What relief and joy when they saw it was an oasis
indeed with springs of water. Gratefully they had drunk
from the well, had filled their containers, and newly
strengthened had marched on and finally reached their goal.

Now in his prayer our pilgrim thinks with gratitude of
that unknown benefactor who once long ago had dug in the
middle of the desert until he came upon springs which had
flowed hidden deep under the sand and rock. So in his
prayer he blesses those who had gone before him through
the valley of Baca and made it a place of springs.

Let us now leave the ancient pilgrims and ask ourselves
what this word may have to say to us. Is it not a parable of
life? How often poets have compared human life with a
pilgrimage, a journey. Sometimes it leads over tree-shaded

roads, through pleasant valleys, up to inspiring mountain-tops—for each human life has a measure of happiness, of joy, of fulfillment. But alas, there are also always the valleys of Baca—the hard and bitter experiences of life, the disappointments, the frustrations, the defeats, the suffering. All of us, sooner or later, have our personal date with trouble. Goethe, the great German poet, at the end of a long life which had been unusually successful, rich in accomplishment, fame, and fortune, wrote: "I cannot think of any period in my life as long as two weeks of which I could say that it gave me unclouded happiness."

This, then, is the common lot of our humanity. But the decisive thing is not what happens to us, but what happens in us; not the experiences that the circumstances of our individual lives bring to us, but the way we accept them and react to them. All of us have to go through our valleys of Baca, but how do we get through them? As I look around I find that various people have different philosophies of dealing with them.

Here is the philosophy of escape. It says: "Keep smiling." You will remember the popular song: "Pack up your troubles in your old kit bag, and smile, smile, smile." Now this is quite all right, as far as it goes. A healthy sense of humor will go a long way in helping us to deal with the small irritations of life. If every married couple learned how to smile and even to laugh heartily at the right time when an insignificant argument threatens to grow into a bitter disagreement, how many marriages would be saved from ruin. Yet you cannot laugh your way through your real troubles. Did Jesus smile when he faced the cup of suffering in the Garden of Gethsemane? Does a mother smile when she sits by the bedside of her child and sees that young life slowly ebbing away? No, life is a terribly serious business. And those who tell us that we can smile away its dark and somber aspects simply do not do justice to its deep seriousness. The butterflies that flutter gaily through the valleys of Baca leave no trace behind them.

Then there are those who try to meet life's difficulties with defiance. They say: "Yes, life is hard and often bitter. But what of it? I take up its challenge; I shall never surrender." One recalls the lines from William Ernest Henley's famous poem, "Invictus":

> Out of the night that covers me,
> Black as the pit from pole to pole;
> I thank whatever gods may be,
> For my unconquerable soul.
>
> It matters not how straight the gate,
> How charged with punishment the scroll,
> I am the master of my fate,
> I am the captain of my soul.

This sounds very brave, and the men and women who have made this philosophy of defiance their own are brave people indeed. But basically is this not merely a negative approach to the problems of life? Surely we must admire people who go through life with "head bloody, but unbowed," but is that enough? Are these not like valiant soldiers marching through their valleys of Baca, giving blow for blow, never whining about their hard fate? Yet, defiance for its own sake is sterile; it produces nothing of lasting value. The footprints of these intrepid souls will soon be blown away by the winds of time, and nothing will remain of them to bless others who will pass this way after them.

Then there are those whom we must call the defeated. How beautiful, how noble were their dreams of love, of great service to mankind, of happiness, of success. But how different life has turned out for them: the slowly turning wheel of daily humdrum, the disheartening setbacks, the sense of utter hopelessness, and finally the bleak surrender to defeat. Now they are just about licked. As Henry Thoreau wrote of them, they live lives of quiet despair. They do not any longer expect anything from life. Like slaves chained to the treadmill of their daily uninspired round of duties, they are trudging along, and often they feel as if they might just as well not have lived at all. They, too, leave no trace behind them in their valleys of Baca for which others may bless them.

But there is still a fourth kind of people. Their lives may contain no less trouble than the lives of their fellow men, their burdens may not be lighter than those of others, but they do not try to smile them away. They do not exhaust themselves in defiance. They do not give up in defeat. Because they believe in God, they are convinced that this God has a purpose and a plan for their lives, and that therefore nothing that happens to them is without some meaning and significance of its own. So they believe that not only their triumphs, but also their troubles must contain hidden blessings. They bend their ears to the ground, listen for the whisper of springs under the sand, and then begin to dig until they find them.

You see, you have here something that is central in the Christian faith: the possibility and power of transformation. Study the whole history of Christianity, and you will see that like a golden thread the conviction runs through it that the valleys of Baca can be made into places of springs.

Sometimes it has been physical suffering. Certainly the apostle Paul knew something about that. Whatever the affliction was from which he suffered, he describes it as a thorn in the flesh, and he says that he felt sometimes as if the messenger of Satan himself buffeted him. So it was only natural that he prayed to be delivered from this scourge. But God says, "My grace is sufficient for you, for my power is made perfect in weakness" (2 Cor. 12:9b). And Paul, realizing that some divine purpose is to be fulfilled in and through his suffering, accepts it, and actually exclaims, "For the sake of Christ, then, I am content with weaknesses" (2 Cor. 12:10a). He has made his valley of Baca into a place of springs.

Sometimes it has been a bitter loss. James M. Barrie, the Scottish playwright, has written a little book about his mother. The first chapter is entitled: "How My Mother Got Her Soft Face." There he tells of the death of her first-born son. Her grief was deep, but it gave her an understanding and gentle compassion for those who had to go through a similar experience. Whenever a mother lost her child and was unable to master her sorrow, the neighbors said to her, "Go to Mrs. Barrie; she knows how you feel; she will help you." And she did. She had learned to transform her valley of Baca into a place of springs.

Sometimes the valley of Baca has been a hard blow of fate, seemingly undeserved and unreasonable. Think of Beethoven, as quite early in his life deafness descended upon him. What a cruel thing to happen to a man for whom the world of sound was everything! At first he rebelled bitterly, and almost lost his will to live. But then he accepted his fate, and while the outward world was silent to him, he heard with his inward ear the power and beauty of an immortal music which he put on paper and gave to the world. One of his biographers wrote about him: "We are eternal debtors to his deafness. It is doubtful if such lofty music would have been created except . . . in the utter isolation this affliction brought about." So here again is a place of springs in the valley of Baca.

Let me emphasize, this is the Christian way of acceptance and transformation. Christianity believes that by the grace of God suffering can be transformed into a blessing; a handicap can become an asset; a disappointment can turn into an opportunity; a cross, "emblem of suffering and shame," can become the very symbol of God's redeeming love. The valleys of Baca can be made into places of springs.

Has not perhaps too much Christian thinking been along the lines of escape and even defeat? Have we not said too often to ourselves, "This is a sinful, evil world, but one day Christ will reign, and then there will be no more sin, no more hate, no more injustice, no more war." That is true enough, and we believe it with all our hearts and long for that time to come. But if we make our Christian hope for the future a means of escape from the tasks and challenges of the present, then we are truly failing in our Christian discipleship. Surely, we cannot even by our best efforts make a perfect society here and now. We cannot transform the whole valley of Baca into a Garden of Eden right away and everywhere. But each one of us can, somewhere, in the middle of the desert of our lives, in the midst of our troubles, create a place of springs from which the clear, clean waters of hope and faith and joy go forth into a world which is so desperately in need of them. It may not be more than a word of encouragement spoken at the right moment to a disheartened person; it may be the taking on of a responsibility in the church from which everyone else seems to shrink back; it may be a service to the community which in a small way will make this community a better place for all who dwell in it.

What have you done with your personal valley of Baca? You may have tried to run away from it, but you soon found out that you could not. You may have become bitter about it, but that certainly did not help either. Why not try to make it into a place of springs? For if it is true, that to them that love God all things work together for good, there must be a hidden meaning and purpose in your trouble, waiting for you with the grace and help of God to discover it and to transform it into a blessing for yourself and for others. Could anything more wonderful be said of us than this: As they went through the valley of Baca they made it a place of springs.

Through Shut Doors

Eight days later, his disciples were again in the house, and Thomas was with them. The doors were shut, but Jesus came and stood among them, and said, "Peace be with you." Then he said to Thomas, "Put your finger here, and see my hands; and put out your hand, and place it in my side; do not be faithless, but believing." Thomas answered him, "My Lord and my God!" Jesus said to him, "Have you believed because you have seen me? Blessed are those who have not seen and yet believe."   —JOHN 20:26-29

☦ IT USED TO BE the rule in Moravian mission fields for the sacristans to close and bolt the church doors when the celebration of the Lord's Supper began. I can still remember the impression this made on me when I first saw it done. No doubt utilitarian considerations lay at the bottom of this custom: late-comers were not to disturb the attention of the congregation during the sacramental rite. But the action also seemed weighted with symbolical meaning. Had not our Lord compared the kingdom of heaven to a marriage, for which the wise virgins were ready and to which

THE RIGHT REVEREND KENNETH G. HAMILTON, President of the Executive Board of the Moravian Church in America, Northern Province

they were admitted, but from which a shut door barred the foolish with such complete finality?

The Gospel reading from John assigned for the Sunday after Easter also speaks to us of shut doors. It tells, however, not of an act of divine judgment but of barriers behind which Christ's followers had sought shelter. That had been a stormy week in Jerusalem, following the day of our Lord's resurrection. Once more the little company of the faithful was gathered behind closed doors—no doubt for fear of the Jews. They certainly had cause to be concerned, since those who had crucified their Master could well be expected to complete their designs and crush his adherents by force.

Doors might shut out others, but they could not keep our Lord away from any who stood in need of him. He appeared among his own that night as the Good Shepherd in search of a single straying sheep. He knew the condition of Thomas, doubting and confused and lonely in the very circle of his friends. Patiently and lovingly Jesus dealt with his stubborn disciple, leading him to full surrender and joyous faith.

Let us consider Thomas as the representative of all those who, though outwardly in the fellowship of Christian believers, lack the assurance which springs from living communion with Christ as their Lord and God. What barriers separate such men from him? We think of only two today, two common causes that deprive some men of the full blessing which others experience as they unite in worship on the Lord's Day.

"Do not become faithless," seems to me the preferred translation for the words our Lord used as he admonished Thomas. This follower of his did not completely lack faith, but he stood in real danger of losing it. Thomas had loved his Master; some two weeks earlier he had proved this by his readiness to go to Jerusalem to face death with him. Like the rest of the disciples he had accepted Jesus as the Christ

sent to redeem Israel. The crucifixion had shaken that faith.
If Jesus had truly been God's great servant, argued Thomas,
how could his ministry have been permitted to end in failure
and death?

Then came Easter with its strange accounts of Christ's
resurrection and of his having been seen alive by certain
of his followers. Such a thing was incredible, said Thomas.
As the days passed and he brooded over these reports, the
issues became clear to him. His friends must have been self-
deceived. He, however, did not intend to yield to wishful
thinking. Why, if this thing were true, then Jesus must be
more than a chosen servant of the Almighty. He must be
Lord of life and death, himself divine. Thomas could not
conceive this to be so and certainly did not expect to encounter his Master in the upper room that night.

So our hearts are often closed to Christ through our failure to expect him to meet us, even though we join outwardly with others in accepted forms of worship which have
brought blessing to men through the years. We recite prayers that lack meaning for us, because we neither let them
possess our inmost thoughts nor expect them to be answered.
They thus have become vain repetitions, against which our
Lord warned his hearers, as against a heathen practice. Have
the words we hear read from the Bible lost their power to
reach our hearts? Do the hymns we sing no longer express
our yearnings and our hopes? Have our acts of worship
grown so familiar that we enter into them without any
thought of their changing us or bringing us face to face with
God? If such is the case, it is little wonder that we remain
lonely and restless among God's people, like blind men set
in the midst of the seeing.

Whenever we cross the threshold of a church, we must
enter in the spirit of Jacob at the ford of the Jabbok, who
wrestled with God's messenger and cried, "I will not let you

go, unless you bless me" (Gen. 32:26b). For the promise belongs to those who hunger and thirst after righteousness that they will be filled. Surely few sins can be so hurtful as our lack of expectancy when we call upon God. In a sense such an attitude becomes an ever-repeated denial on our part of the resurrection and the living presence of our Lord.

The trouble with Thomas, however, lay not in the weakness of his faith alone, I believe, but also in the stubbornness of his will. Consider the grounds he had for accepting the account of the resurrection as true: Trustworthy friends of his testified that they had seen and communed with the Lord. Two of them had walked with Jesus to Emmaus. To them the Lord had expressly interpreted the things recorded in all the scripture concerning himself. They must have repeated his words again and again to all who cared to listen to them. Thus Thomas should have understood much that had been hidden from him before, both truths contained in the writings of the prophets and certain sayings of the Master himself, by which he had sought to prepare his followers for his passion and death. Thomas would remember with new insight the occasions on which Jesus had spoken in his own hearing of what the third day would bring. If his Master were risen indeed, then this simply confirmed what he had repeatedly foretold.

It seems to me that Thomas that night must have been like Paul on the road to Damascus, long after, "kicking against the goads," to use the inspired phrase. Surely he was consciously resisting inner conviction. Instead of yielding to the testimony of his own heart, he stubbornly demanded proof from the Lord which he had no right to ask: "Unless I see in his hands the print of the nails," he said, "and place my finger in the mark of the nails, and place my hand in his side, I will not believe" (John 20:25b).

All too often we follow the example of Thomas in this respect as well. We are not ready to yield our wills unreservedly to the leading of the Holy Spirit. We would not have him take complete control of our lives. Search your hearts and see whether you have not often recognized that it was your Lord's will for you to confess him in some definite way, or to yield him obedience in some specific situation. Then, because you were not fully surrendered to him, you resisted his leading, professing to need added certainty as to whether the inner voice had divine authority or the word of scripture had reference to you. You, too, sought for signs and proofs to reinforce what in your heart of hearts you knew to be your God-given duty. To persist in this course is to shut a door which effectually keeps the Savior out of your life.

The Gospel reading does not speak of Thomas alone, however, but also of his Savior. Christ's coming to Thomas proclaims that divine love is not easily daunted by man's little faith or stubborn willfulness. The Lord did not reject Thomas despite his weakness and sin. Of Christ it is written: "If we are faithless, he remains faithful" (2 Tim. 2:13a).

The very need we have of coming together for worship week after week in the house of God, may hinder us, I think, from realizing the blessed truth that in reality it is not we who first seek God, but God who in his infinite compassion has sought us. True, the scripture encourages us to be concerned about the state of our soul and to turn to the Lord in conscious awareness of our dependence upon him. "Ask, and it will be given you; seek and you will find; knock, and it will be opened to you" (Matt. 7:7). But all our searching would be vain if God had not first sought us. It was necessary for the prodigal to come to himself and return to his father's house, but that would have availed him little, if the father had not long been waiting, ready to welcome him home.

Indeed, the parable of the prodigal can suggest the reasons for this interplay of the divine search and the human in our redemption. The fifteenth chapter of Luke records three parables. In the first our Lord tells of the shepherd seeking his lost sheep; in the second, of a woman searching for her lost coin. In both of these the initiative lay entirely with the owner, whose concern it was to repossess property that had been lost. No question arose under such circumstances as to the willingness of the animal and the piece of silver to being restored to their rightful owner. But in the third parable the father coveted more than the physical return of the prodigal. Even had he been able to discover his son's whereabouts in that "far country" or to compel him by force to return, such an act would have been self-defeating. Until the unhappy youth became aware both of his own need and of his father's goodness, no true reunion was possible, no meeting of hearts. Therefore, the son had to "come to himself" before he could be "found."

In dealing with man God respects our freedom, so that our love may be unconstrained by anything other than his own. Therefore, we read in the book of Revelation that Christ is content to stand at our heart's door and knock. Yet thanks be to God he does come and knock long before we are ready to yield our pride and admit him. Yes, God has sought us; therefore, and only therefore, are we able to seek him. The mark of the nails in Christ's hand and of the spear in his side speak to us of the lengths to which God went in his search.

Jesus Christ abides as the Great Physician of souls. As he knew the needs of Thomas, so he is aware of the state of his church and of each one of us who calls upon his name within it today. No door of circumstance can shut him from us, though it lies in our power to reject him. We have his promise: "Where two or three are gathered in my name, there am I in the midst of them" (Matt. 18:20). If then we are aware of weakness and sin in our life—the shortcomings which burdened Thomas or any others—we may trust in the all-sufficient grace of our Redeemer and open our hearts to heed his word: "Blessed are those who have not seen and yet believe" (John 20:29b). If we learn to pray, "I believe; help my unbelief," we too shall find peace for our hearts.

This sermon began with a reference to a custom which I had seen in the mission field. Let me close it by describing an unusual plant which we came to look for each fall in tropical America. Our people called it the resurrection lily. Late in the year the bulb would send up its leaves, waxy, heavy, luxuriant leaves. After some weeks they died away, and the plant showed no further sign of vitality. The spot gave no indication that any life remained hidden beneath the surface there. Then, without warning, usually about Easter time, out of the bare earth came lovely little flowers, that looked somewhat like our crocuses. To me, that plant symbolizes the event to which our thoughts have been directed.

By God's goodness and mercy Thomas not only learned to believe in the resurrection, but, because of his doubts and struggles, gained a deeper understanding of what the resurrection meant than any other of the Twelve. To this disciple for whom Easter came a week late, the church owes its shortest creed: Jesus is "my Lord and my God."

A World of Value

And the world passes away, and the lust of it; but he who does the will of God abides for ever.   —1 JOHN 2:17

O A FORMER CLASSMATE of mine in Bible study at Lane College selected as his subject for a paper at the end of the school year "Man in Two Worlds," which upon reflection he changed to "Man in One World," which later he made to read "Man in One Aspect of the World." His still later decision was to let both Man and the World alone and write about something else. He finally did the former, but not the latter.

The late Wendell Willkie was well informed about Man and the World, and from time to time had much to say about both, and he would do this in varying forms. After his last world-encircling trip he came home and hurriedly compiled and published his *One World* and shortly thereafter took his departure from it.

Paul Hutchinson, for many years a close student of the world in its changing moods and a realistic writer, in his concluding article of a series written during ten months' travel and observation around the world, discusses the world

---

DR. J. ARTHUR HAMLETT, Bishop of the Christian Methodist Episcopal Church; President of Christian Service Center, Inc.

as fact and possibility. It is not two worlds about which he writes, but two ways of looking at this one world. Among other things he says: "The world as fact is a terrifying, doom-threatening reality which no informed mind can dismiss. The world as possibility is something that may be missed amid the alarms of these days. Yet this latter conception is the ground of our hope and it is the responsibility of religion to insist on its existence."

Let it be said that "science is a regulated system of facts" or a method by which we discover the world of fact; or call it whatever may comprehend and simplify a task. Science, then, is concerned with facts and is best functioning when it is discovering, organizing, and classifying facts. If the world is in a great quest for facts it is the function of science to find them. Through the aid of science we may know what the facts are about the physical world and physical man, and if we do not understand them we cannot blame science; and if we do not properly use them for the expanding and enrichment of the world and the elevation of mankind, science itself cannot be held responsible. If we make slow progress in the matter of full and complete living in a universe with fair knowledge of it, what could be expected of us in complete ignorance of it? It is the business of science to tell us what the facts are in the world about us. How to behave in the possession of the facts, what to do with them, how to manipulate them toward any desired end, how to adjust ourselves to them so as to make the most of living—all of that lies outside the realm and strict functions of science.

If a certain arrangement and experimentation of atomic energy will result in the destruction of life and property in a given community, is it not the function of science to inform us by investigation, organization, verification, and demonstration? But whether such ought to be done is a question we should not ask of science and chiefly for two reasons. First, it is not the function of science to tell us what ought to be done or what ought not to be done; second, we can and do find instruction on that question from another source. It is the function of science to inform us as to the composition of stone, its age and weight and even the velocity with which it may be hurled through space. But whether such a stone should be hurled in a fashion so as to bruise my head or to crush the head of an innocent child is information we either already have or can easily get, and whether we seek such information or not it is available, and will be offered free of charge if too many stones begin suddenly and unexpectedly to fall upon heads cut out for other and more noble purposes.

Science can tell of facts the organization and manipulation of which may lead to inventions that make a high-powered Packard car available for my use or yours. But whether that car should carry one on an errand of vice and crime or to innocent amusement or the house of worship, we certainly would not ask science. Because of the constant and engaging service science has done, and is still doing, we find ourselves today living almost in a new world; new not only in the sense that creative processes are still operative, but also in the sense that man's real world after all is the world that he knows and with which he has some kind of relation.

The constantly increasing knowledge which science has, and is giving us, presents us a new world. It is not the same world that our fathers knew for they lived in a world which man's thought could easily handle. History could be covered by a small span that stretched only four thousand years back of Christ. At the center of the universe was the earth, and around it the sun, moon, and stars made regular visits for man's convenience and delight. So if a certain battle was to be decisive before sunset the captains could either hurry along with the battle or request the sun to wait until the battle ended before going down. All of this caused no apparent violation of laws—partly, because there were very few laws to violate, and partly because if the natural laws demurred against such infraction the supernatural laws could take over the program without any violation. Modern science has changed all of this. It now requires scores of thousands of years to cover the history of man, and of course the globe is older than that, by ages.

The earth itself is now only a tiny fragment of a vast universe. The sun, which is now the center, is a million times larger than the earth, and that sun is one of the least among a thousand million suns that make up our galactic system. Miles cannot now very well measure the universe, so vast has it become in the facts discovered by modern science. The swiftest movement we now know is the passage of light one hundred and eighty-six thousand miles in a second, and eleven million miles in a minute. Yet there are stars so distant that the light which started from them before the pyramids were built has not yet arrived at our earth, and beyond our galactic system are other systems of like size; the nearest is so far that a million years is hardly time enough for the swift-spreading light to travel to our globe.

In addition to pushing back the walls of space and time, science has informed us of a world of the unbelievably small. In this new and vaster universe is the story of the microbe, the world of life hidden from sight. Add to this the story of the atom—no longer some last, lifeless particle of matter as older science thought, but itself a universe with its electrons moving in their regular orbits and its being throbbing with energy. As H. F. Rall would say, "All this, however, is only, as it were, the framework of the new world. Even more important, is the new way of looking at the universe and conceiving its ongoing life. This new conception is indicated by three words: evolution, order, and dynamic."

The universe is not something fixed and unchanging; with distant suns, with life on earth, with the very chemical elements with which this earth is made there is the same story, the story of continuity and change. What is, has come out of the past and will in turn, give way to something else. Individuals, nations, planets, suns—all have their course of birth, growth, and decay. The second word contains the idea of order—order everywhere, and mere chance nowhere. The duty of science is to discover this order, the way in which things behave or what we call the laws of nature. The third word, "dynamic," tells the rest of the story. The old world of dead and lifeless matter is gone. Reality now is energy, power, and power to do. Such is the world that modern science brings to us. Are there any values in such a world? Do we need another and different teacher to inform us regarding the world of value?

One definite conviction that affects a large area of study and reflection today is that man's faith in the Christian religion has imposed a terrific strain upon the knowledge that must support that faith, that a vigorous morality must be fed on a quality of intellectual food which does not reward indifference to the vast area of knowledge available for man's guidance. The fact that Christian religion is good, wholesome, uplifting, and saving is no reason for any lack of adequate understanding of what it is, of how effective it may be in the world, when allowed freedom that simple intelligence can give.

If man's scientific progress has multiplied his problems, he needs to remember that comparable moral and religious progress would multiply his strength and equipment for meeting and solving those problems. Henry R. Luce has said, "Man's technology has outrun man's morality." That should suggest that man move forward a little faster in his moral desires, ambitions, and growth. This will come when more people get the notion that moral and religious progress, with all its attendant wonders, is at least a grandchild of the church, having come out of the European civilization which the church largely created. Today, it is said, science and technology are greatest where Christians are most numerous.

Modern Christians cannot separate themselves from the world that science has revealed. The economic, social, political, and ethical power in the world today is largely Christian. What is needed is that the Christian religion take a new look at the world, bring itself up to date regarding the factors at work in it, understand something of the functions and relationship of those factors, and then assume its place of leadership in a world that is alive and moving, with the understanding that leadership means some understanding of what is to be led, and the various factors and influences involved. This will require, among other things, exponents of the Christian religion who know the difference between being in front—pointing the way, and lagging behind—trying to find the way, or in the middle—blocking the way.

Science is primarily concerned with facts; religion is concerned with values. Through the aid of science man has discovered himself and his world. Through religion man has discovered the world of value, and how to live in it. His success at the former has been amazing; his slow progress at the latter has created his baffling and stubborn problems. Science has, undoubtedly, aroused new interest in this world, and seeks to keep us more aware of the changes taking place. Let us hope that religion has become more constructive in its attitude toward everything that concerns this world, whether scientific, social, or historical.

As representatives of the Christian religion, let us come to a fresh and vigorously working understanding of the functions of both science and religion, and then apply that understanding to the world situation that calls for a leader-

ship with adequate program to meet the world's needs. The
Christian religion is the program! Involved in it is the wisdom, technique, and courage to organize all the facts and
influences, to utilize all the light and knowledge, and to
channel all the powers required to make this world a para-
dise of God where all his children may live together as a
loving family.

The Christian church must know and teach that there
is a world of value, and that it is not the province of science
to deal with it. The structure of earth, science may describe,
but not its grandeur or its beauty. Science is expected to tell
about the age of rocks, but not about the Rock of Ages—
except, possibly, by implication. The Christian religion
must tell that! About the growing grass and budding flowers,
science must tell, but the world will know little or nothing about the lily of the valley until the poets and prophets
sing and preach! About the bones and muscles and blood of
man, science can tell, but not about his character! Religion
tells about the world of spirit, of persons, ideals, and values.

Science may inform us regarding the formation of the
earth; religion tells us who formed it. Science may inform
regarding the ascending gradations of animal life in the
evolutionary processes that finally resulted in man, but the
Christian religion speaks of man as a living soul, and classi-
fies him not among the animals, but among the angels. He
was made a little lower than the angels.

In the world of value there is beauty, there is truth, there
is goodness, there is justice, there is love, there is happiness.
This world offers us life's highest goods and deepest mean-
ings. This world comes to us not so much with a demonstration, but with a challenge—a challenge to behold the
beauty in Christian character, and to go forth to make more
of it in the world; a challenge to behold the beauty of the
Lord, and to inquire in his temple; a challenge to walk

about Zion and round about her, tell the towers thereof, mark well her bulwarks, consider her palaces, that we may tell it to the generations following.

In this world of value, science is a stranger and the tools of the scientist cannot function. Beauty may be talked about, but cannot be measured. Physics may describe the nature of light—the laws of refraction, and the interfering elements in the atmosphere as illustrated at sunset—but the beauty of a sunset and its glory lie wholly beyond its ken. So chemistry may tell you of the salt, and iron, and sulphur, and the rest that go to make up man, but what this added something is that we call *life*, it cannot tell, and still less, what this man is in terms of reason and character, of friendship and loyalty; what he is as a personal being, as a man. Yet, it is just this in which we are most interested!

The world with which we are most concerned, after all, is the world of persons and values, of man and God, of love and truth, and beauty, and goodness, and justice! If, then, modern science has acquainted us with this newer and vaster world of physical fact, the Christian religion has taught us regarding the world of value, the world of spiritual reality. The poet and artist, saint and seer, have always known a world of spiritual reality, and have not waited for permission of science to believe in it. The higher values of life find a creative source in something that is basic in the universe. There is, therefore, a ground of hope for their survival.

Mission of the Church —
So to Act

THERE IS NOT A WORD in the Bible about the American
Board of Commissioners for Foreign Missions, or the
International Board for Missions, or the Council for Christian Social Action, or the National Council of the Churches
of Christ in America, or the Division of Life and Work. Yet,
there is a sense in which these constitute the subject matter
of practically all the Scriptures. "To him be glory in the
church" (Eph. 3:21a). The church is to give glory to Christ.
It is not an end in itself. It has an instrumental character.
It has a task to fulfill.

Hendrik Kraemer summed up the matter in these words:
"In its missionary outreach, in the discharge of its missionary
obligation, the church reveals its deepest reason of existence:
that is, to continue the ministry of Christ in the world."
Read scripture's best witness to God's revelation in Christ
in words like these: "God was in Christ reconciling the world
to himself" (2 Cor. 5:19a); "God so loved the world that

DR. FRED HOSKINS, Minister and Secretary of the General
Council of Congregational Christian Churches; Co-president of
the United Church of Christ

74

he gave his only Son, that whoever believes in him should not perish but have eternal life" (John 3:16). Or read words like these: "All authority in heaven and on earth has been given to me. Go therefore and make disciples of all nations, . . . teaching them to observe all that I have commanded you" (Matt. 28:18b-19a, 20a); "that through the church the manifold wisdom of God might now be made known" (Eph. 3:10a); "But you shall receive power when the Holy Spirit has come upon you; and you shall be my witnesses in Jerusalem and in all Judea and Samaria and to the end of the earth" (Acts 1:8). Or observe what happened when the women personally experienced the resurrection—they ran to tell others; and what happened when the men of Emmaus personally experienced the resurrection—they ran to tell others; and what happened when the disciples experienced the resurrection—they ran to tell others; and what happened when Paul experienced the resurrection—he ran to the end of the Roman world to tell of it; and whatever since has happened when men have known by the grace of God that there is an Easter in the world—they have not ceased running back and forth across the earth to testify, "He is risen," and that he goes before men to their Galilee. Come at it as you will, you can scarcely avoid the conclusion that when you treat of the church you are dealing essentially with an enterprise which is functional. It has a mission to accomplish: to be a better witness to Christ, and that by continuing the ministry of Christ in the world.

If the church is to be a better witness to its Lord there are indeed some implications of how it is to conduct itself. For one thing it is incumbent upon the church *so to act* that the world will find in its actions an endorsement and authentication of what it professes with its lips and presumes in its interior being.

Apparently it is commonplace for a court of law to accept the words of a dying man as unassailable truth. But if a man is not departing this life immediately he has to do more than talk if he is to be believed. His testimony of words has to be supported in some way that will corroborate them. His actions are the best possible endorsement.

The obituary notices of the demise of the church have proved to be gross exaggerations. The church is still alive and talking. It is not near enough to its death to have its testimony accepted without challenge. And that is very serious for the church, because the accomplishment of its mission depends upon its being believed. Somehow the church has to bring the world to believe that its testimony to the resurrected Christ, and to the Father of our Lord, is true.

How in the first place was Jesus verified as the Messiah? To an impressive extent what he said with his lips was confirmed by what he did. A man who has been blind from his childhood is inclined to believe every word that falls from the lips of the one who restores his sight. The person tormented by seven devils is almost certain to believe anything said by the one who gives him peace of soul. The sinner who burns in a hell of remorse and droops in the loneliness of separation from God is going to believe what is said by the man who, with no discernible ulterior motive, opens for him the door to forgiveness and oneness with the Eternal.

The Master understood all this. When John sent his disciples to learn whether or not Jesus was the Messiah, the Master did not equate his authentic character with any word he might say but directed: "Go and tell John what you have seen and heard: the blind receive their sight, and the lame walk, lepers are cleansed, and the deaf hear, the dead are raised up, the poor have good news preached to them" (Luke 7:22b).

For the authentication of Christ there was an inherent

persuasiveness in the words he spoke, but the really con-
clusive factor was in the action of God. It was, for example,
what God did in the resurrection that provided an endorsement of him as the Word which was to be communicated to
the world, obstruct and thwart as men might.

Is it not clear that if the church is really to be Christ's
church it is incumbent upon it so to act that the world will
discover it to be authenticated by what it does? The world
will believe, or not, what we say about the love of God and
the dignity of man and the excellence of justice and freedom
depending upon what we do where men are divisive or fearful or unjust or in want or in ignorance.

The church will be authenticated to the world, depending
upon how it acts in response to God's prompting toward worship and fellowship and unity and witness. If the church be-
haves as if it were only a particular cultural penetration of
a pagan suburb or an inner-city ghetto or an African labor
compound or a legislative hall, its word will go no farther
than the ears of the hearers. If on the other hand it so acts
that the world sees that indubitably the church is a divine
penetration it may, like Jacob, respond: "Surely the Lord is
in this place; and I did not know it. How awesome is this
place [this factory, this office, this suburb, this mine, this
tribe, this school, this race, this people, this land]! This is
none other than the house of God, and this is the gate of
heaven" (Gen. 28:16b, 17b).

Then must the church so act.

To continue the last thought with a bit more emphasis I
will suggest that it is incumbent upon the church so to act
that the world may *never* mistake it as solely a product of the
culture in which it exists. Even if one had never read H.
Richard Niebuhr one would surely find it easy to believe that
the church as one knows it in any part of the world is ex-
tensively fashioned by the culture surrounding it. So we

have middle-class churches and labor churches and wealthy churches and united churches. They exhibit much the same kind of organization and program as other groups within the community.

The church has succeeded only too well in demonstrating to the world how much it has in common with the luncheon clubs and the country clubs and the patriotic societies and all the other features of a fascinating, if not satisfying, culture. In making clear that it surely is *in* the world it has confused many by failing to contradict their understandable error of believing it is *of* the world.

Ah, but when the church is true church it decidedly is something other than an organism which chameleon-like reflects whatever is in the contemporary culture. Think of it this way: Take away from the church militant all the features which may be accounted for by man alone and by his culture. Take away its buildings and its money and its economic and political and social organizations. Take these and all other purely cultural deposits away. The church will appear very different. Some would not be able to recognize it as the church. Possibly some would not even know old First Church if it did not have its annual fall bazaar, or its exclusive, sectarian sorority to which "the girls" have been going on Tuesday afternoons since they were in high school forty years ago. But take them away and there remains an impressive body of mystery.

The remaining mystery is the very life of the church. It is all that really counts. For what is left is the same mystery of which Paul exclaimed, "Great indeed, we confess, is the mystery of our religion" (1 Tim. 3:16a). Did he mean that our religion is unknown and unknowable? Not at all. He meant just the opposite. He was pointing to the mystifying greatness and goodness of God who from the very beginning destined us to be his children, and in whose love and purpose there was a Word which long was unknown but now was fully and wonderfully known for, as he continued:

> He was manifested in the flesh,
> vindicated in the Spirit,
>   seen by angels,
> preached among the nations,
> believed on in the world,
>   taken up in glory (1 Tim. 3:16b).

It is incumbent upon the church so to act that the world can never mistake it simply as a manifestation of a cultural phenomenon engaging, like other familiar organizations, in self-aggrandizement and the exploitation of the realms outside itself. Like its Lord who gave his life for it, it must be confronted by the world and found giving its life and actually and effectually breaking down the walls which partition men from one another and fence them off from God.

It is Christ in the church who gives the power for the pursuit of this kind of ministry.

One summer I put my boat in the water very late in the season. This was not due altogether to a delinquency in effort. Actually I first put her in early in the season, but she nearly sank. I took her out and put on another coat of copper paint and pressed in a bit of putty at points of obvious need. I put her in again and once more she leaked like a sieve. Grounded the second time I calked her well, so I thought, with prime quality, honest-to-goodness calking. But back in the water she leaked about as much as ever. I would deceive myself no longer. There was a fundamental fault in my boat and I was trying to cope with it with too easy solutions. What the boat needed was basic treatment. She needed some new planking. And when she had it she began to behave as a boat.

It is incumbent upon the church so to act that the world will believe that in it is the radical treatment meet for man's predicament. Not every one knows how to describe it, not all understand it, but just about every thoughtful person is aware that contemporary man is caught up in a king-sized predicament. Books and plays and music and suicide and murder and wars and threat of wars and sputniks and tons of tranquilizers and oceans of liquor, all speak eloquently, if not inspiringly, of the predicament of man.

One day in New York I was one of three and one-half million people who were "destroyed" by an enemy atomic bomb. But we were not destroyed in that cruel game, until we were chased into bomb cellars and subways and other unpromising places of safety. We had gone into our places of hiding because we were threatened with arrest if we did not go. Having gone I supposed we were saved until I read in the papers afterward that we had been killed anyway. Suppose we had not wanted to go underground to get saved? Well, society required that we be saved in any event. The irony of the experience was that being supposedly saved we were destroyed notwithstanding. The greater irony is that every last one of us who was destroyed knew what would save us all— not to drop any bombs. It all points to the terrible predicament of man: He knows he needs to be saved, but unaided he cannot find salvation. He needs a Savior.

Characteristically, man has been trying to resolve his very fundamental predicament by recourse to solutions too easy, too simple, and too evil. "Build up bigger military machines." "Build more schools and colleges." "Get out the vote." "Be the first to put a man on the moon." Recently on a plane a seatmate with all seriousness proposed to me that Congress should, on some equitable basis, appropriate billions of dollars to the churches for their missionary work in foreign countries, especially in Russia and her satellites. This, he affirmed, would quickly effect the destruction of communism and all would be right with the world.

The church is as guilty as any of presenting too easy answers for too complex problems. "Join the church—just say, 'Lord, I believe.' " "Think positively." "Go to church." "Pray daily for peace." These are too easy answers for the predicament in which man finds himself.

It is incumbent upon the church so to act that the world will see instantly, and believe, that it is something more basic than a tranquilizer or a stimulant. Man must be able to see by its actions that the church is a radical treatment meet for his terrible predicament, that it takes man as he is and confronts him with the Eternal who destined him for sonship. Man must be able to see by its action that the church reveals the good news of a divine event through which God bequeathed forgiveness and freedom and life eternal. The church must so act that the world does find in it a nerving to live above the circumstances of a grave predicament, and to do so as sons of God.

The human side of Jesus was irritated by his church. "It is not for you to know times or seasons which the Father has fixed by his own authority" (Acts 1:7). But the divinity in him was manifest when in an instant he continued, "But you shall receive power . . . and you shall be my witnesses in Jerusalem and in all Judea and Samaria and to the end of the earth" (Acts 1:8).

For better witness, it is incumbent upon the church so to act that "Christ is formed in all mankind and every land is thine!"

What Type of Christians Are We?

They all look after their own interests, not those of Jesus
Christ. —PHILIPPIANS 2:21

WHAT TYPE OF CHRISTIANS are we? This question is justified by the condition of our society. All the Christians
of our age "look after their own interests, not those of Jesus
Christ." This is true, regarding not only the laity, but also
those who profess that they do look after the interests of
Jesus Christ because of their zeal and Christian activity.

Since the day that the soldiers divided the garments of
Christ (John 19:23) at the base of the cross on which he was
giving up the spirit, until today, those who have been guard-
ing Jesus have continued to look after their own. Nothing
has changed.

Christ is nothing less than the Signal, the complete calling
in all our "ecclesiastical" endeavors. Woe to all of us, if a
penalty were imposed each time the name of God was used
in vain. We would be among the most condemned, because

THE MOST REVEREND IAKOVOS, Archbishop of The Greek
Orthodox Church of North and South America

82

as "churches" we continually disguise our sins under the pretext that we are laboring for Christ.

We not only fail to seek those things which are Christ's; we fail also to seek those which are our own as Christians, because as Christians we should seek nothing more than Christ and that he be the Vine and we the branches. Of our own we have no life; he is the Life. But how many of us who preach him as our Savior and Redeemer and who over-emphasize faith, can truly describe ourselves with the words of Paul: "The life I now live in the flesh I live by faith of the Son of God" (Gal. 2:20b)?

Do we as churches do anything better in the present situation? The answer to this question is given by today's reality. Never have there been so many efforts by churches to approach one another as in the period following the last World War. All the churches have embarked on ecumenical movements. All the churches are striving and seeking with anguish to find themselves closer to other churches. They all stand firmly, however, on their own grounds waiting for the others to make the move, because they seek their own and not the things that are Jesus Christ's.

Thus we are confronted with an ecclesiastical condition that could not claim a better title than "nonecumenical ecumenism." The ecumenical movements are steadily becoming less ecumenical and are in danger of being drowned in the shallow waters of denominational ecumenism. I would say that it is time to have a personal reappraisal, but I do not dare, because only the "spiritual man" can appraise and judge all things and consequently himself (1 Cor. 2:15). Are we spiritual men in the sense that Paul states, or are we rather "natural men"? I ask this question because "we impart this in words not taught by human wisdom but taught by the Spirit, interpreting spiritual truths to those who possess the Spirit" (1 Cor. 2:13).

To convince ourselves as ministers of this fact it is not necessary to refer to books, periodicals, newspapers, or the sermons of others. Our sermons, our discussions, our words, as well as our deeds are sufficient. How much of the Spirit of God is truly in our sermons? How many of us seek and ask for the things which are of Christ Jesus and not our own?

I am afraid that the Christians of the present era are in the category of those children described by Jesus in the eleventh chapter of Matthew: "But to what shall I compare this generation? It is like children sitting in the market places and calling to their playmates, 'We piped to you, and you did not dance; we wailed, and you did not mourn'" (16-17).

We belong in this category not only as individuals, but also as churches, because of the meaning we give to the word church in our day. If you do not like the term "childish Christians," try to find a comparable one, but in essence that is what we are. When we do not look after our own interests directly, we look after them indirectly to the tune of "We piped to you, and you did not dance; we wailed, and you did not mourn."

The result of our partitive tactics and polity is that we have kept ourselves isolated and distant from Christ to such a degree that we have commenced to wither (John 15:6). We manifest symptoms of such spiritual stagnation that we are today threatened by a separation from the Vine, and not by the hands of Christ (that would be right), but by the hands of each other or those of the invisible enemies of Christ.

To the latter, we ourselves many times give shelter. We harbor within us not only partitive and separatistic tendencies, but ofttimes our thoughts are so rationalistic and secular that in essence they are not different from the materialistic beliefs of the ungodly and the antichrists. When we do make efforts not to convey this type of impression, we become so general, so indefinite in our expressions and our polity, so indefinite in quality, terming ourselves, for instance, "religious cosmopolitans," "free-thinkers," "liberals," and "friends of peace," that we do not differ at all from the enemies of Christ and Christianity. This is what happens when we forget the teachings of the Lord as he meant them: "Do not think that I have come to bring peace on earth; I have not come to bring peace, but a sword" (Matt. 10:34).

I think it is time to return to the proper order of things, and as the foremost principle of this most important endeavor, I would like to return to the question, "What type of Christians are we?" Primarily we owe it to ourselves to supply the answer to this question. Are we Christians of Christ, or Christians of the churches to which we belong, and consequently Christians who seek their own and not the things which are Jesus Christ's? If we are of Christ, we are also of his church, because the church is Christ himself; not the invisible Christ, but Christ, who yesterday and today is the same, and unto the ages, Christ who emphasized that "he is not God of the dead, but of the living" (Matt. 22:32b).

In speaking to the faithful of Corinth, Paul says, "Now you are the body of Christ and individually members of it" (1 Cor. 12:27). Paul gives two more descriptions:

"There is one body and one Spirit, just as you were called to the one hope that belongs to your call, one Lord, one faith, one baptism" (Eph. 4:4-5).

"You are . . . members of the household of God, built upon the foundation of the apostles and prophets, Christ Jesus himself being the chief cornerstone, in whom the whole structure is joined together and grows into a holy temple in the Lord (Eph. 2:19b-21).

The Christians of Christ do not derive life from other sources. Life stems from their faith in him. He emphasizes this faith and bond in John 6:53b: "Unless you eat the flesh of the Son of man and drink his blood, you have no life in you."

The Christians of Christ are in constant contact, in the closest of bonds and in continuous unity with Christ. This is their chief characteristic. The Lord testified to this truth: "He who eats my flesh and drinks my blood, abides in me, and I in him" (John 6:56).

The Christians of Christ draw their inspiration only from the words and teachings of Christ. The Lord himself demands this: "The words that I have spoken to you are spirit and life. But there are some of you that do not believe" (John 6:63b-64a). I am afraid that we, the Christians of today, believe not and for this reason we seek our own rather than the things which are Jesus Christ's.

My purpose is not to end with this conclusion, but rather to use this conclusion to urge the commencement of a new journey by Christians and by churches with a profound and complete cognizance of our obligations as Christians. It is imperative that we journey toward the cross, which casts very dark and heavy shadows upon us as it did upon those who crucified Christ. We must journey toward the cross and kneel before this holy symbol, not to cast lots for the garments of Christ, but to see if we are able to guard and avoid tearing the coat of Christ (John 19:24).

When we see that the coat continues to remain one, woven from the top throughout (John 19:23), we must make efforts to be clothed with this coat. Let us seek to clothe our nakedness and let us try to warm our hearts with the warmth of Christ, with the warmth that comes as a result of unity in Christ after having finally clothed ourselves with Christ. "For as many of you as were baptized into Christ have put on Christ" (Gal. 3:27).

Only when we have really put on Jesus, can we hope that we shall truly seek the things which are Jesus Christ's.

The Quest for Spiritual Abundance

And when he had ceased speaking, he said to Simon, "Put out into the deep and let down your nets for a catch." And Simon answered, "Master, we toiled all night and took nothing! But at your word I will let down the nets." And when they had done this, they enclosed a great shoal of fish.

—LUKE 5:4-6a

✝ "PUT OUT INTO THE DEEP and let down your nets for a catch." Jesus does not rebuke the fishermen because of their past failures. He simply commands them to go out again where the water is deep. He does not command them to go to another sea. He does not direct them to get new boats or new nets. They are to go out upon the same sea in the same boats and to use the same nets.

In this age of haste and speed we are often tempted to worship change, and frequently act as if a few failures dictated that we look for new situations, forgetting that there are still many new and unrealized possibilities in old situations. There are some, for instance, who would desert the United Nations Organization because it has failed to bring

DR. J. H. JACKSON, President of the National Baptist Convention, U.S.A., Inc.

peace to the world after ten years of trial and error. But it has many real achievements and great political and moral potential, and we believe that men and nations should continue to use this organization to develop international understanding and good will, to secure justice, and to assure peace.

I say to those American citizens who hunger and thirst for justice and for a fuller freedom, you need not turn away from this great republic or seek to destroy its structure and life, or to break its laws and to sin against its lofty principles of freedom. The Constitution of the United States, the doctrine of democracy, and the American ideals of liberty are sufficient to give and to guarantee every American citizen the goals that his heart desires.

The organized church has made and is still making some great contributions to the uplift of human society. Yet we are frequently appalled at its many failures, and hasten to repent of all its sins. But the past errors of the Christian church are not sufficient grounds for us to desert all of its principles, its ideals, and its promises. We do not need a new Bible, a new Calvary, a new plan of salvation, a new Christ, or a new gospel. These are ancient goods, but the times have not rendered them uncouth. In spite of political and social revolution, in spite of the new knowledge that has come in our atomic age, society has not outgrown the ethical standards proclaimed in the gospel of Christ. We need to make a more thorough and creative use of these available means of grace; for there are new possibilities, new moral and spiritual insights available to mankind through a more serious approach to the Christian way of life.

On December 5, 1959 I sat for eight hours in a conference with atomic scientists in the city of Chicago. I was shaken as I heard them tell the story of the destruction that would come in the wake of an atomic war. What was the only possible defense against such a war? Their unanimous conclusion was that the only hope for men is in the moral field—to learn how to live together observing the principles of justice and good will, and putting aside the vices of hate, envy, and strife. It seems that the call today is not to the church alone but to the whole world to launch out upon the deep seas of moral and spiritual possibilities and make strenuous efforts to find practical means of living together in peace. For we must risk all for peace, or lose all in war.

Like the ancient fishermen, we are confronted with many failures. We have fought two world wars within a generation and there are those who say there is no escape from a third world war. There are those who regard man as a hopeless sinner, depraved beyond recovery and eternally lost, and the victim of the evil forces of the world. But we must not allow the disappointments of the past to blind us to the possibilities of the future.

In response to this command of Jesus, Simon Peter did not say that it was useless to try again. He and his companions had tried and failed, but they did not make their failure determinative. They had struggled for a whole night. When the long hours of the night yielded to the radiance of dawn the story was the same as it was at the beginning of the venture—they had nothing. Fortunately for Peter and those that were with him, he did not say after the night's toil, there was nothing. He simply said, "We toiled all night and took nothing." The failure of a whole night was long, but all too short to exhaust the resources of the sea. Because they had caught nothing, they did not say there was nothing.

How often we ascribe too much power and authority to past failure! We overtax our knowledge, overwork our ignorance, and act as if what we do not know were sufficient ground to support a whole philosophy of life. Men have written doctrines of atheism and have assumed the right to outlaw all religion and to reduce the Christian faith to the level of fable and fancy because of what they do not know and cannot prove by physical test and measurement. There is a school of thought which contends that because the heavens have been searched by telescopes and no God has been found, therefore there is no God. Let astronomers probe as deeply as possible into stellar dust, name the stars of the heavens and count them one by one, trace the orbit of gyrating planets and measure the course of whirling galaxies, and let modern scientists defy the laws of gravitation and go voyaging to the habitation of the moon and plant man-made stars in the open spaces of the skies. Yet, they will not know enough to deny the revelation of the psalmist and to negate his vision: "The heavens are telling the glory of God; and the firmament proclaims his handiwork" (Ps. 19:1).

What if geologists have unearthed silent stones and read on the faces of ancient rocks the stories and wonders of the ages and eons of the earth. They cannot conclude from this that there is no Christian Rock of Ages. Depth psychologists have probed into the mental life of mankind, surveying the pale domain of hidden phobias, unconscious and frustrated drives; observing the very citadel of demons and the breeding places of moral and social corruption. Yet, these findings do not justify the conclusion that man has no soul, no inner life, no disposition to rise above the animal level of human existence and to live a life after the dictates of the Spirit of God.

In November, 1959 a group of scientists gathered at the University of Chicago to celebrate the one-hundredth anniversary of the publication of Charles Darwin's *On the Origin of Species by Means of Natural Selection*. Among those present were Charles Galton Darwin, the grandson of Charles Darwin, and Sir Julian Huxley, the internationally-noted biologist from London, England. Speaking at the convocation, Huxley predicted, "All religions are destined to disappear to make way for a new order of thinking." As a biologist, Huxley has made a great contribution to the scientific thought of our age, but when he ventures to prophesy regarding the future of religion, he overworks his imagination, leaves his lofty position as a scientist, and sinks to the level of the ordinary mind lost in a fog of dogmatism and speculation.

All of the knowledge and accumulated wisdom of the ages is but a night compared with the boundless resources of the universe and the fathomless wisdom of God. One night's experience is not enough for us to conclude there is nothing of the great spiritual values for which the Christian church stands. We have not accumulated enough knowledge to answer in the affirmative the great questions of the writer of the book of Job: "Can you find out the deep things of God? Can you find out the limit of the Almighty? It is higher than heaven—what can you do? Deeper than Sheol—what can you know?" (Job 11:7-8)

In the story of the text Peter and his companions confess that they have toiled all night and taken nothing. "But," says the spokesman for the group, "at your word I will let down the nets." In spite of past failures, and notwithstanding the limitation of their own powers, Peter and his companions decided to accept the words of Jesus and act accordingly.

Karl Barth has ably pointed out the supremacy of the Word of God over the word of man in the work of redemption. We rely on the Word of God as our hope for full salvation. Of course we would not reduce man to the level of an automaton or a spineless and irresponsible victim of the divine will. We do not accept a determinism that robs man of the freedom of choice. Man can will to follow the way that the Master leads, but man does not have the power to determine what that way shall be. It is the Word of God that has laid out the plan of salvation. It is the wisdom of God through grace that has set before all men an open door of eternal hope. It was God who set up the cross as the way by which the lost could be found, prodigals could return to their father's house, and the guilty could be cleansed from all sins and unrighteousness. But man must will to accept what God has given him or be left eternally in the pit of ruin and in the gall of bitterness. Therefore, if we would be saved from our sins, we must accept God's plan, obey his command, and trust his Word. Peter said: "But at your word I will let down the nets."

The powerful church of yesteryear was the church that took seriously the Word of God. The vital church of the present age is the church that puts faith in the Word of God beyond the theories and speculations of men. The most dynamic and creative church of the future will be the church that walks not by sight, but by faith in the eternal word of God. We must say as Peter said: "But at your word I will let down the nets." In spite of past experiences, in spite of our sins and our human depravity, we will accept the divine orders and sail in the direction given to us by the divine Mind.

Real religious experience always goes beyond profession to practice, from confession to commitment, from creeds to consecration and deeds, from theory to thrust, from interpretation to encounter with reality. A vital faith leads to a vital life. "Faith apart from works is dead" (Jas. 2:26b).

Peter and his companions went beyond a mere statement of intention and put into execution the Master's command. They went out into the deep and let down their nets for a catch. Luke says: "And when they had done this, they enclosed a great shoal of fish" (5:6a). When they had obeyed the Master's command, when they had put faith in the Master's words beyond the testimony of past failures, when they had risked all on the directives of Jesus, when they had done this, they enclosed a great shoal of fish. The reward comes after the venture. If we would know the doctrine of Christ we must do his will.

The psalmist teaches the reward of the venture of faith when he says, "Some went down to the sea in ships, doing business on the great waters; they saw the deeds of the Lord, his wondrous works in the deep" (Ps. 107:23-24). In all matters pertaining to the spiritual life, we must push out from the ordinary and the commonplace, and go out by faith upon the great seas of divine promises and do business in the deep waters of spiritual possibilities. Only those who take such a venture will see the works of the Lord and comprehend his wondrous deeds of love, mercy, and redemption.

Do we expect to experience the blessings of eternal salvation and to enjoy the fruits of the Spirit? If so, we must do what the Master says—repent of our sins, confess him as Lord, deny ourselves, surrender our pride, and humbly take up his cross and follow him.

The American Board of Commissioners for Foreign Missions which was the first missionary society in America, did not come into being from a committee on resolutions. It grew out of the old haystack prayer meetings conducted by Samuel J. Mills and other young men of dedicated spirit at Williams College. These men turned from a narrow nationalism and sectarian thinking, to a higher and more inclusive quest. They ventured forth to preach the gospel to men and women of the heathen world. They lifted their hearts Godward, and they resolved to venture into unknown lands, not for conquest, not for material gain, but for the purpose of carrying the gospel of Christ to men and women beyond the seas. And when they had done this, the vision of God broke upon thousands of souls in other lands and men and women turned to the light of truth and found a new fullness of peace and joy.

The Baptist Missionary Society of England came into being
in the latter part of the eighteenth century. It was the result
of the dedication and commitment and missionary passion of
William Carey and those who worked with him. In preaching his famous sermon in the Baptist Chapel at Nottingham,
England, Carey uttered these memorable words: "Expect
great things from God; attempt great things for God." He
dramatized in his own life and experience that expectation
was not enough. Men must attempt to do the things that God
requires. When Carey had done this a new spirit of missions
swept across the unbelieving world and the kingdom of God
moved forward.

The genesis and history of all great Christian movements
and achievements may be traced to the lives and spirits of
men who have made their commitments to God. Bishop
Charles Brent, one of the great moving spirits in the modern
ecumenical movement, believed profoundly in "unity in
diversity." He believed that the basic principles of Christ
were the foundation on which all believers could firmly
stand. He believed that the best approach to unity was
through a life of prayer and through acts of turning toward
God for guidance. Brent once said, "Those alone labor effec-
tively among men who impetuously fling themselves upward
towards God." When men fling themselves up towards God,
or risk their fortunes on a venture of faith, they come to
moments of great creative power.

In 1948 when delegates from all parts of the world were
converging on Amsterdam, Holland to organize the World
Council of Churches, one young man of Amsterdam was
heard to say, "Just think, people are coming to our city from
all over the world and Christ brings them here!" I can never
forget the glorious moments of the opening service of this
first assembly that took place in the Nieuwe Kerk at Amsterdam on Sunday, August 22, 1948. One hundred forty-seven

churches in forty-four different countries were represented by three hundred fifty-one official delegates. It seemed that one could almost hear the words of Christ in his intercessory prayer: "I do not pray for these only, but also for those who are to believe in me through their word, that they may all be one; even as thou, Father, art in me, and I in thee, that they also may be in us, so that the world may believe that thou hast sent me" (John 17:20-21).

In the spirit of venture and faith, peoples of different religious denominations, different languages, and different nationalities sought the deeper things of the spirit and went in quest of a more creative fellowship among the Christians of the world. And when they had done this, when they had ventured into the deep waters of divine possibilities and had let down their nets the result was a new birth of unity among the Christians of the world.

The time is at hand, and the Christian church is summoned to launch out into deeper and more inclusive ventures with Christ. In this dark hour of the world's history, mankind must embrace the light of Christ. Robert Browning in his "Paracelsus" expresses the faith that is essential for our time:

> If I stoop into a dark, tremendous sea of cloud,
>   it is but for a time:
> I press God's lamp close to my breast;
> Its splendor soon or late will pierce the gloom;
> I shall emerge one day.

The age of the gospel has not passed, and the hour for a great venture of faith is at hand. Will we desert the task, or will we move forward to a victorious venture?

The Unity God Has Given Us

There is one body and one Spirit, just as you were called to the one hope that belongs to your call, one Lord, one faith, one baptism, one God and Father of us all, who is above all and through all and in all.   —EPHESIANS 4:4-6

WE BELIEVE WITH PAUL that we are all one in Christ Jesus. Therefore we are joining in this service of worship. This oneness is a given fact. The one God and Father of us all, who is above all, and through all, and in all, has called us to himself in Christ. This is what the church is essentially: a body of people summoned by God to hear his word, to receive his life, and to do his will. We are one people, members of the one body of Christ, and we come together in joy and gratitude that it is so.

Yet we are divided, and because of this also we are here. By your presence here, you are saying that you believe there must be greater mutual understanding among Christians of

THE RIGHT REVEREND ARTHUR LICHTENBERGER, Presiding Bishop of the Protestant Episcopal Church in the United States of America. This sermon was preached at a union service in Morristown, New Jersey in which seven denominations joined.

different denominations, that we must know one another and our differing ways better, that we must work together as much as we can as Christian people. But even as we affirm our oneness in hymn and prayer, even as this service is an expression of our desire to become what we actually are— one body—we are separated. We are not in full and open fellowship. We who are one in Christ do not manifest that unity to the world. So we come, not only in thankfulness that Christ is not divided, but also in penitence for our disunity.

These are the realities of our situation in the church in our time. We are one, yet we are divided. We could not be gathered here at all if we were not one body in Christ. It is of the utmost importance that we know this and never forget it. I must say that now and again as I have sung, "We are not divided, all one body we," and then thought of the number of separated churches we have in this country, almost three hundred, I have wondered about that hymn. But we are one body even though we have separated ourselves from one another. Over twenty years ago in Edinburgh at the second Conference on Faith and Order, an affirmation of unity was made. "We are one," those Christians said, "in our Lord Jesus Christ the incarnate word of God. This unity does not consist in the agreement of our minds or in the consent of our wills. It is found in Jesus Christ himself."

This is the unity God has given us. We did not make it, we can only receive it, and enter into it by God's grace. We are one body, but now it is up to us to become what we are. This is the obedience to which God calls us.

Twelve years ago the Church of South India came into being. United in this one church are people who formerly were Methodists and Presbyterians and Congregationalists and Dutch Reformed and Anglicans. It took an incredible amount of patience and charity, forbearance and faith, to accomplish this. For twenty-eight years representatives of the various churches prayed together, talked together, and worked together. At times the difficulties before them seemed insurmountable, but they persisted. Finally they reached agreement. The Church of South India was born.

How did those who had labored so long for this accomplishment look upon the union? As their own work primarily? Here is a story which gives the answer. It is told by Marcus Ward in his account of the first years of the Church of South India, which he calls the "Pilgrim Church." He begins with a story about Bishop Azariah, the great Indian Christian who worked so passionately for the reunion of the church. "No one who heard it will ever forget the agony in the voice of Bishop Azariah as he told how a large and promising movement toward Christ came to nothing because the inquirers discovered that united in Hinduism, they might well be divided in Christianity. 'We proceed no further.' " Dr. Ward ends his story of the beginning of the Pilgrim Church with another conversation between a Christian and a Hindu. This Hindu gentleman "speaking sadly about the bitterness and tension which marked the first five years of the Republic of India said to a member of the Church of South India, 'But you have done what we could not do.' So the story which began with Bishop Azariah's tragedy a few years ago has come full circle. Would that the great Indian Christian had been alive to hear this. But comment cannot rest here. '*You*,' said the Hindu. No, not *we*. It is the Lord's doing and it is marvelous in our eyes."

The Church of South India is not a human device. It is not the creation of a new church out of fragmentized, unrelated parts of churches. It is for a million Christians in the land of India the recovery in part of the visible unity of God's church, and it is the Lord's doing.

There is a stanza in one of our great hymns which I must confess I cannot bring myself to sing: "Rise up, O men of

God! The church for you doth wait, her strength unequal to her task; rise up, and make her great!" No, we cannot do that. Jesus Christ is the church's one Foundation, and the greatness of the church is solely in the glory of the Lord. There is much we can do, of course. God will not do for us that which we can do for ourselves, but it is utterly beyond us to make the church great, and as we cannot make the church great, neither can we make the church one. Unity is not something which is to be fashioned and put together by us. The church of Christ in its essential nature is one as Christ himself is one. Our part is to let the Holy Spirit lead us into that unity, so it will be evident in what we are and what we do. Our part is to become what we are.

This is the first reality which makes such a service as this possible. There is one body and one Spirit. But then there is that other fact which is so plain to see: our disunity. It is this, too, which brings us together today. We have broken our unity in Christ and how greatly our witness as Christians is weakened because we are divided. One of the proper marks of a Christian, I believe, is the mark of deep mental and spiritual unrest because we are divided and do not manifest our unity in Christ our Lord.

One man speaking of Africa, put it like this: "It is no good saying with a passionate gleam in the eye, there is one solution for Africa, one faith, one Lord, one baptism, and then moving at a snail's pace about church unity there where there are 269 registered Christian denominations. There is a problem for God's community." Quite as true for us here, for every land, but we are so used to our divisions, some of us, we take this as so natural and so much a part of the ecclesiastical scene that we are not disturbed or shocked by it. It is much more evident for what it is in countries where Christians are very much in the minority. There is a story told about an American traveling in northern India. As his train stopped at a station he saw an Indian distributing religious tracts. Discovering that the man spoke English, he asked him, "Are you an Indian Christian?" and the man answered, "No, I am a Canadian Baptist."

This, then, is our situation. We remember always that we are one in Christ Jesus but we can never forget that through our disobedience and sin we are separated from one another. Because we are one we never lose hope. Because we are divided we are determined to become what in Christ we are: one body worshiping one Lord.

Now since this is the way things are, every act of cooperation between the churches is of the greatest importance. We have come a long way in the last thirty or forty years in the formation of local, state, and national councils of churches, and in the establishment of the World Council of Churches. Then there is that stirring of the Spirit which we call the ecumenical movement. This has affected all the churches, some more than others, but even the Roman Catholic Church, which has stayed aloof, is touched by it. All this as Archbishop Temple has said, is the "great new fact of our time."

I believe that every one of us can have a part in this. In fact it is quite essential that people in local congregations be involved. Church unity does not come through the efforts of a few clergymen and lay leaders. We must all desire it, pray for it, and work for it. And if we want the church to be united, if we pray for it, what more can we do? Well, this for one thing: If you are a Presbyterian know as much as you can about your own church, its distinctive traditions and teachings, its particular gifts. Do not be an indifferent Presbyterian or Methodist, if you are one, or Episcopalian. For I am sure of this, that a Presbyterian, for instance, who understands the tradition of his own church, values it and loves it, and an Episcopalian who loves and understands and values his church, are much better equipped and ready for serious conversations about church unity, ready for what is called an ecumenical encounter, than two people who know little and care little about their own inheritance. A member of my church who attended a union service in another church one time, said to me afterward, "I don't see why we can't get together without all this talk. I can't see what it is all about. These differences don't amount to anything." He did not know what he was talking about. The things which divide us are not superficial, and we cannot overcome our divisions by saying they are not there.

One of the unexpected results of the conversations and encounters between separated churches these past thirty years has been that these churches have become more aware of their own distinctive characteristics. As one man who participated in a number of conferences on Faith and Order said, "We came together to get to know each other, only to find that often we did not know ourselves. Called upon to give an account for our separateness, we discovered the distinctive teachings of our fathers in the faith."

If we see the coming great church not as a theological compromise nor as the absorption by one church of all other denominations, but as the bringing together into one by the Holy Spirit the gifts and the treasures we now nurture separately, if this is the unity we look for, we can prepare for it by being informed and loyal members of the church to which we belong.

Then there is this. We can ask God to take from us "all hatred and prejudice and whatever else may hinder us from godly union and concord." I do not know how much hatred there is, but I know there is much prejudice—prejudice which closes our hearts and minds against the truth. You know the story of the two men who belonged to different churches. They had a long discussion about their different denominations, arguing with each other as to which was the true church, and finally one said, "Very well, you worship the Lord in your way, and I'll worship him in his." We can, as we have the opportunity, if we have the mind and the will, come to learn and appreciate the value and traditions of churches other than our own.

And one more thing. We who belong to separated churches must have faith strong enough to look at our differences clearly, and explore those differences. This is difficult; this takes time. If you were to read the detailed account of the conversations in India which lasted twenty-eight years, and which resulted finally in the Church of South India, you would see surely that this required much faith and patience and courage. We who have deep and differing convictions on matters of faith, on the nature of the church and the ministry, must be ready to face our differences with the intention and the hope that if we do confront one another in truth and in love, we may be led by God into a manifest unity. As one great ecumenical leader of our time has said, "What is needed at the present time of ecumenical encounter is not to be as sweet as possible with each other, but to learn the art of being as true as possible with each other." Speaking the truth in love, yes, and hearing the truth in love. I am certain that this kind of confrontation among us is good and necessary.

So I hope this service today is a symbol of our awareness of who we are and what we are called to do. We are members of one body, yet through our blindness and sin we are divided. We are brought together both by our oneness and by our disunity. We are called to repentence for the sin of division and we are called to pray and work for the visible unity of the church of Christ. May we be kept together by God's grace and be led by him into that unity which belongs to the people of God.

The Personal Element in Unity

✝ WE ARE IN A PERIOD of the ongoing life of the church when great stress is being laid upon the unity of those who are professed followers of Jesus Christ. Let us thank God for this emphasis! Let us not say as did a sectarian representative in a group in which I participated some time ago, that all unity talks and efforts are but signs of the apostasy of the church, and a mark of the last days.

Rather let us find in what is taking place that guidance of the Holy Spirit which is bringing us face to face with the need to think, to pray, to work, to adjust and readjust, as we are confronted by the implications of it all. I know of nothing that can so well serve the purposes of God with us as individuals, congregations, and church bodies, to jolt us, jar us, and shock us out of the narrow sectarian and parochial ways of thinking and acting which are ours so often. In the light of the demands upon us every time we face a unity discussion, we may discover that all too often we have been motivated, not by the love of God, take us where it will, but

DR. MALVIN H. LUNDEEN, President of the Augustana Evangelical Lutheran Church

by the love of denominational grouping, and by the attitude, "I dare anyone to disturb me in it."

Let us therefore "plow deeply" in this field, by the study of the Scriptures (not least, Paul's letter to the Ephesians), by reading books and articles, and joining with others in fruitful discussion of the unity theme. Let us pray for the guidance of God so that our concern be, not for some interesting academic discussion, but rather for an actual personal facing up to the demands with which we should be confronted every time we approach this matter of Christian unity.

Basic to any consideration of this matter is a fact we dare not minimize, that is, natural man as a person is in a state of estrangement and separation. First of all, he is separated from God. This separation is the essence of sin, for it has come about by the exercise of man's self-will. We are sinners, not because we break the Ten Commandments. Rather do we break the Commandments because we are sinners, that is, in an unreconciled relationship with God.

It is at this point that Christ attacks our problem. His atoning work on the cross, and his Easter victory provide the means whereby our estrangement can be brought to an end, and reconciliation effected with God. Paul puts it in these words: "God was in Christ reconciling the world to himself, not counting their trespasses against them" (2 Cor. 5:19a). His gifts of grace, forgiveness, life, and reconciliation with God are received by faith alone. You do not achieve or earn them. You appropriate them by faith, which is as an empty hand stretched out to receive. And it is God who works even the faith, as Paul reminds us: "For by grace you have been saved through faith; and this is not your own doing, it is the gift of God" (Eph. 2:8).

Second, natural man is separated from his fellow men. That is why it is so easy for us to eye one another with suspicion rather than with confidence. That is why we all too often look upon our fellow men to *use* rather than *serve* them. That is why it is so easy for us to establish our caste systems, which exist not alone in India but pretty much throughout the world, including our own United States of America. That is why there are among us those who think of themselves as "first class" citizens, and who look upon others as "second class" people. This is true not only in the Southland, but in the Northland as well.

But if Christ's atoning work has had its opportunity with us these barriers between man and man are broken down, too, even as those between man and God. By his redemptive, sanctifying work in us, he transforms us, and our attitudes. Is this not what Paul means when he writes: "Therefore, if any one is in Christ, he is a new creation; the old has passed away" (2 Cor. 5:17a)?

In other words, Christ, in redeeming us, reconciles us to God as he binds us to himself by faith. In him we are incorporated into his body, the church. We are brought under his lordship. By that act, not our own, but God's in Christ, we are brought into fellowship and communion with all others, who, in faith, have come into the same experience and relationship.

Therefore it is not only possible, but also absolutely necessary, to say that unity is a gift from God in Christ Jesus our Lord. We do not create unity, or achieve it, any more than we produce God's forgiveness of our sins. It is God who brings to an end our separation and estrangement, not only from himself, but also from one another. Our problem in this whole area is the problem of discovering for ourselves, personally, that which already exists.

This two-sided principle, that unity is God's gift and that our part is to become aware of it, needs to be well established in our hearts and minds, for it will provide that direction in our unity discussions that will keep things on an even keel. Too often unity is thought of in terms of organizational and promotional schemes to which we must give our assent, much the same as the efforts which produce NATO, or the United Nations, or a federation of women's clubs. Nothing is further from the truth! It is this superficial concept which has produced the enthusiasts in the name of church unity whom someone has labeled "ecumaniacs." Perhaps too, if we would recognize unity for what it is, God's gift to us in and through Christ, we would be far more ready to admit how stubbornly sinful we are in our failure to live in the fullest expression of that unity.

Often we hear references to the scandal before the world of our divided state as a church of Jesus Christ. When we understand unity to be what it really is, the gift of God to us, we will realize that the scandal is not so much in that we are divided among ourselves as Christians. That is bad enough! Rather does the scandal become so much the worse when we must recognize that our divided state is an evidence of our failure as Christian believers to accept what God is offering us—his gracious gift of unity. How we plead with those who turn their backs upon God's gifts of faith and forgiveness. Should we be less concerned about our own failure, and that of others, to see and to accept this gift of God's grace?

But, though God gives unity and unity thus exists, it is not perfect in our present world. Far from it! This imperfection is not in the gift, nor does it come because the Giver is withholding the gift. We must face the sober and convicting fact that it is we—stubborn, willful mortals that we are, even as Christian believers—who are the obstacles to an adequate expression of the unity in Christ, either by our indifference to this gift of God, or our blindness at this point (we just cannot see it), or by a deliberate rejection of it.

So there must be efforts and movements seeking to bring about a discernment of this gift of God, and an acceptance of it, by an ever increasing number. In such discussions many factors are involved. There are doctrinal differences, the seriousness of which must never be minimized. The principles of church polity and administration are many and varied. We cannot escape dealing with them. There are differences among Christians which exist because of traditions, reflecting a variety of geographical and nationalistic distinctions. These, too, must be faced and given proper evaluation.

Perhaps, however, our concern for the problems of theology, polity, and tradition has caused us to overlook another important factor, one which comes a little closer home to each one of us. I am referring to Paul's exhortation to the Ephesians in which he urges the readers of his letter to be "eager to maintain the unity of the Spirit in the bond of peace" (4:3). There will be little or no advance in getting people to discern God's gift of unity unless those engaged in the task possess an eagerness to maintain that unity in the bond of peace made possible by the Holy Spirit. Here is a personal call for "lowliness and meekness, with patience, forbearing one another in love" (Eph. 4:2). So important is this matter of attitudes that Paul indicates that only as we possess right attitudes will we "lead a life worthy of the calling to which [we] have been called" (Eph. 4:1b).

How eager are we to maintain the unity of the Spirit in the bond of peace? That is a question which must be answered by the individuals who make up the groups involved in unity. It is a personal question. As God's gift of unity is received by ourselves, and as we are busy helping others see and accept it, we cannot possibly escape the very personal element involved.

The New Commandment

"A new commandment I give to you, that you love one another; even as I have loved you, that you also love one another."

—JOHN 13:34

THE CONTEMPORARY WORLD is passing through a crisis. The struggle for existence and the hectic pace of life seem to be driving us toward perdition. Man's penchant for physical acquisitions, for pleasure and entertainment, his passions and hatreds are carrying him as a powerful flood toward the abyss of pagan materialism. Men are prone to forget the God of love and goodness, the gospel of truth and justice; they reject the immortality of the soul, since it cannot be proved by their physical senses. Men turn their eyes away from Christ's banner of peace, and raise instead the banners of hatred, bloodshed, and crime.

Such is the picture before us today. Men have strayed away from Christ's commandment of love, and have withdrawn from Jesus the Savior of the world. What is the attitude of the so-called great and small Christian nations toward his gospel?

If we look upon the external, superficial aspects of contemporary life, we shall answer: "Is it not true that we pos-

ARCHBISHOP SION MANOOGIAN, Primate of the Diocese of the Armenian Church of America

sess thousands of magnificent churches, armies of clergy? Is it not true that every Sunday from thousands of lofty steeples, church bells toll their invitation to the faithful to come to the house of God, and from within come the harmonious sounds of hymns, chants, and the reading of the Scriptures? Then why be so pessimistic as to assert that men have alienated themselves from Christ's gospel of love?"

Surely there exist everywhere men of true faith, but, alas, the Christian spirit has become weaker in the hearts of most of the people. Why is this so? Because modern men do not really believe in God, they do not love Jesus with a sincere heart, but worship him with their lips, just as was declared by the prophet Isaiah: "For they worship me with their lips but their heart goeth astray from me."

If we asked someone whether he loved Christ, his unhesitating answer would be, "Of course I love Christ." And if we were to ask him whether he practiced the commandments of the gospel of salvation, he would be confused: he would say, "Do you have in mind the Decalogue?" The answer is no, the *new* commandment, the commandment of love! For the Savior of the world is the God of love. "A new commandment I give to you, that you love one another; even as I have loved you, that you also love one another" (John 13:34). But we do have many things to love—our relatives, friends, family, fatherland, and especially, ourselves, our ego, money, wealth, property, comfort, and pleasure. We have many idols to worship, false gods, besides the true God.

But let us see what Christian love is. What does love mean in the true Christian sense of the word? It would be well nigh impossible to define the love, the providential love, of Jesus. The crucifixion of Christ, even though wordless, explains magnificently God's love. So stated John, the evangelist of love, in explaining the incarnation of the Son of God: "For God so loved the world that he gave his only Son, that whoever believes in him should not perish but have eternal life" (John 3:16). This is the measure of God's love. Jesus is the personification of the divine love. His name is Love, as one of our Armenian church fathers, Nerses the Graceful, wrote: "Jesus whose name is love, soften thou my stony heart with thy love."

Christian love is the perfection of life; he who has love becomes a repository of all virtues. It is the salt of the earth. Without love the world would become altogether corrupted. Until men learn to love one another, evil cannot come to an end in the world. Passions and hatred debase men, lowering them to the level of beasts, but love ennobles and raises them to divine sainthood. Jacques Bénigne Bossuet, the great French preacher, says: "Let us resemble God, for he permits us to resemble him in saintliness." Jesus came to raise men from their position of fallen sons to that of saints.

Christian love is that golden stairway which leads men to God. It is the divine link connecting the world to heaven. The apostle Paul said that of the three virtues—faith, hope, and love—love is the greatest.

Love is God's greatest characteristic, for we cannot say that God has faith since he is omniscient, that he hopes, for he is omnipresent and omnipotent and perceives everything. But we say that God loves, for God is love. He loves his prodigal sons, for he is the loving Father of all humanity.

Then what is the condition of love set forth by Jesus? It is very clear and definite: "If you love me, you will keep my commandments" (John 14:15). The Lord himself commanded: "You shall love the Lord your God with all your heart, and with all your soul, and with all your mind. This is the great and first commandment. And a second is like it, You shall love your neighbor as yourself. On these two commandments depend all the law and the prophets" (Matt. 22:37b-40). But who can love another person as himself? This commandment can be accomplished only in the Christian spirit, by loving our fellow men as the Father loved us, with a supreme sacrificial love, whereby he sacrificed his only begotten Son for the salvation of the sinful world.

"Greater love has no man than this," said our Lord, "that a man lay down his life for his friends" (John 15:13). Truly, the greatest natural love is one's self-sacrifice for another. But still greater than this is Christian love, vaster and more infinite. Here is what the God of love commands: "Love your enemies" (Matt. 5:44b). What, to love one's enemies? But, that is impossible! We hate our enemies and wish to do them harm. The concept seems to be contrary to man's nature and instinct—of course, when man is considered only as a physical being. We love only our beloved ones, our friends, and not our enemies and those who hate us. Who can fulfill this impossible commandment? Is this not the greatest of all paradoxes?

Yet, if we look at this commandment with utter seriousness, we find here the distinct superiority of the Christian religion over the other religions. If we believe that we are brothers and the children of God, which is the basis of Christianity, then there exists no enemy. Therefore we must love our enemy, who is none other than our prodigal brother, just as God loved us, his erring children.

The world has tried every method to secure justice, peace, and happiness—to remedy the trials, miseries, and injustices —but has despaired of ever achieving its goal. Science, inventions, the arts and artifacts, wealth and the enjoyment of material pleasures, new social and economic doctrines and socialist systems, and especially brute force and tyranny—all have been tried without avail. For there exists no all-curing remedy for the ancient evil, but the sole antidote—Christian love, Christ's gospel of love and brotherhood.

It is essential that the flower of Christian love and goodness be planted and cultivated by all the nations. It is necessary to foster the principle of the fatherhood of God and the brotherhood of men throughout the world. For only when nations, peoples, communities, and individuals adopt the redeeming principles of the divine religion, will the kingdom of God establish its reign in the world as it reigns in heaven. Only then will peace and justice prevail upon the earth and men will love as brothers in peace and contentment on this planet.

Let us remember the Lord's new commandment and the question which he thrice addressed to Peter: "Do you love me?" (John 21) If we love him, let us then keep his commandment, which is to love our fellow men, as he loved us.

Eternal Fellowship

You were called into the fellowship of . . . Jesus Christ our
Lord.
                                                    —1 CORINTHIANS 1:9b

✝ ONE OF THE WORST MEANS society uses to punish an individual for wrongdoing is solitary confinement. To note
this is to recall the human need for fellowship. Life would
be incomplete if not impossible in a social vacuum. Abundant life, life at its fullest and best, is rooted in fellowship—
fellowship which is made perfect and eternal through Christ.

The fact that man is a creature in need of fellowship is
brought to our attention in the first pages of the Scriptures.
Following the creation of Adam, God, according to the
record, observed, "It is not good that the man should be
alone" (Gen. 2:18b) and so he created woman as a help-
meet for man. Human fellowship was thereby instituted in
addition to the fellowship with God which already existed
for the welfare and happiness of mankind. Creation was now
complete.

To this day man has not outgrown the need for social
interaction. Of course the character of our association has
not remained so simple and limited in scope as it was with
Adam and Eve in the Garden of Eden. So widespread and

THE REVEREND DANIEL J. MAREK, President of the Synod-
ical Committee, Unity of the Brethren

varied have become our relationships that the human personality is to a considerable extent the product of a maze of social experiences and contacts. We are not only individuals, but individuals who are sons, daughters, husbands, wives, neighbors, employers, employees, church members, and countrymen. Through the various social, religious, economic, fraternal, and political groupings opportunities for fellowship have been greatly multiplied and expanded.

But the truth is that even this great variety and number of social relationships does not assure experiences of fellowship in the best sense, the type for which we have been created and for which we have a real need. In fact, the greatest aggregation of human beings can produce the deepest experiences of loneliness. The reason for this can ultimately be traced to the shadow that fell over that first fellowship in the Garden of Eden—the shadow of sin. Disobeying God broke fellowship with God and brought a loss of vital communication of man with man. The results were false witness, mistrust, indifference, envy, and hatred culminating in murder. Fellowship was exchanged for separation and division. Separated from God, man attempted to make his own divinity; divorced from his fellow man, he lapsed into the isolation of self-centeredness—generation upon generation. The broken relationship has continued to blight man's soul created for fellowship.

But all was not lost. "God was in Christ reconciling the world to himself" (2 Cor. 5:19a). Although man chose to turn his back on God in willful satisfaction of his prodigal tendencies, God has remained faithful. In spite of self-righteous pride which has caused man to persist in turning a deaf ear to the entreaties of his Father to be reconciled with his brother and to enter into the joyous fellowship of the Father's house, God has not abandoned him to his own fate. Rather, as the apostle Paul reminds us, "God is faithful, by whom you were called into the fellowship of his Son, Jesus Christ our Lord" (1 Cor. 1:9).

The fellowship to which we have been called in Christ is something more than that which exists among persons engaged in vital communication. How so? It is a Christian fellowship, an experience that is reserved for believers in Christ. It is a relationship of those who have a common heritage to share and a glorious message to bear. In its ideal sense, it is a fellowship of the reconciled bearing the message of reconciliation.

The formal embodiment of this relationship is, of course, the church. The church is the people of God who have given heed to his call. It is an assembly of those who share a common faith in the God of love who has chosen to forgive the penitent in Jesus Christ. The assurance of that forgiveness has awakened in the hearts of the forgiven a desire to say thank you to God for what he has done, is doing, and can do through Jesus Christ. They have come to know that it is in the church that this blessed heritage can be best understood, appreciated, and expressed.

How well our Lord understood our need can be seen in his establishment of the church, as well as in the other phases of his life and ministry. The church was established to serve as the home for babes in Christ. It is, in fact, the place wherein new Christians are born. Every soul needs the environment of the church home even as the child needs a family home. More and more we have come to realize the importance of a good home in the normal development of children and the prevention of juvenile delinquency. In a sense, the church has been established for spiritual delinquents in need of a good home. It is in the church that we come to experience love, understanding, concern, forgiveness, recognition, security, and the purpose of God in Christ as nowhere else. We have been called to such a fellowship.

The mission of the fellowship of the reconciled is to proclaim the message of reconciliation. The best efforts in proclamation often fail, however, because of the lack of reconciliation within the fellowship. As Nietzsche once said of the followers of Christ, "His disciples would have to be more saved if I am to believe in their Savior." Because the church is a communion of saints who are both saved and being saved, the dross that still needs to be refined often gives a false impression of the value and desirability of that which is within.

Perhaps the church has not always sufficiently emphasized the close connection between the life of its people and the effectiveness of their testimony. It has been even less sensitive to the negative impact of denominational divisions upon the world. At its worst, it has been something on the order of what William Taylor describes in his book, *The Parables of Our Savior*. One day while visiting in a town in Scotland, he called upon a friend there who belonged to one of the little denominations which had broken off from a large one on some scruple of conscience. During their conversation Taylor said, "Tell me, how is your church getting on?" With a twinkle in his eye and a smile on his face the friend replied, "Oh, our church seems to have been born for illustration of the infinite divisibility of matter, for there are now forty-five members and seven churches."

The greatest fault has not been so much the existence of a variety of members in the body of Christ as the division among them. To paraphrase what Lincoln is reported to have said about common people, "God must have loved denominations, because he made so many of them." Although there is reason to doubt that God intended all the denominational divisions of the church that exist today, the other extreme would likely be contrary also to his will.

A certain variety of constituent members of the body of Christ can perhaps be justified along the same lines as the composite authorship of the Bible. The truth that God had for mankind apparently required the channel of a variety of human temperaments and experiences. Man's natural tendency to select, to emphasize one thing at the expense of another, makes a variety of denominational emphases necessary in order that the whole truth of God be contained, preserved, and transmitted. Harmony and cooperative effort among the various members of the body of Christ, however, are indispensable if the purpose for which the church exists is to be accomplished.

The church has not always remembered that its chief purpose is to continue the mission of Christ in relation to the world—to seek and to save that which is lost. It has too readily forgotten that its effort must be spent in seeking the other sheep, and this as defined by the truth of God and not by the sin and ignorance of man.

The fellowship to which we have been called in Christ, then, provides us with the atmosphere in which we can grow in grace as it extends to us the privilege of being laborers together with God for the salvation of the world. It is also a fellowship which transcends time and the grave. It is a fellowship which is eternal. From the earliest times Christians have repeatedly affirmed their faith in the "communion of saints." There is no hint that the statement of belief is to be limited to earthly fellowship. The weight of scriptural evidence indicates quite the contrary. The writer to the Hebrews says: "But you have come to Mount Zion and to the city of the living God, the heavenly Jerusalem, and to innumerable angels in festal gathering, and to the assembly of the first-born who are enrolled in heaven, and to a judge who is God of all, and to the spirits of just men made perfect" (Heb. 12:22-23). This is written to Christians as yet in the earthly existence, but it speaks of communion with those already departed.

And why not? As Christians we believe in the immortality of the soul. Fellowship even in this earthly existence, in the final analysis depends mainly upon the vital communication of the spirit, or the soul of man, and not the body. Therefore since the souls of our departed fellow believers are preserved in Christ, and since we have been called to a fellowship in him, although the character of the fellowship changes in death, the fellowship of Christians is eternal.

It is said of Joseph Parker that when his wife died, reflection brought him to the realization that there remained open to him either of two responses to his great loss. One was that of gloomy silence and grief. The other was a determined and, in some sense, a heroic effort to continue in what his wife thought was his best work for both God and man. That which enabled him to make the latter response, by the grace of God, was his firm conviction in the spiritual connection with the departed—that communion in the spirit really takes place. Later he comforted a friend who also had lost his wife by telling him of his own experience. He said to his friend, "I never come to my work without asking my wife to come with me and help me in the strength of God's grace to do it. And she comes."

What a blessed privilege it is to be "called into the fellowship of Jesus Christ our Lord," now and forever!

Discern Ye the Lord's Body?

☦ IN THE ADMINISTRATION of the sacrament of Holy Communion we receive Christ's own words of invitation, "Take, eat . . . this do . . ." Why then should I speak of warning, of judgment? Why should you listen? Because the scripture which invites us to the Lord's Table so speaks. And we must hear its word honestly: "Whoever, therefore, eats the bread or drinks the cup of the Lord in an unworthy manner will be guilty of profaning the body and blood of the Lord. Let a man examine himself, and so eat of the bread and drink of the cup. For any one who eats and drinks without discerning the body eats and drinks judgment upon himself. That is why many of you are weak and ill and some have died" (1 Cor. 11:27-30).

Can what was given for food become poison? Can the "cup of salvation" have opposite effect and become "damnation"? Was the illness—even death—that Paul notes as something unusual in the Corinthian congregation, tied to their mis-taking of the Lord's Supper, as he flatly says? Is

---

DR. JAMES A. MILLARD, JR., Stated Clerk of The Presbyterian Church in the United States

the feverish, enervating activity so easily observed in Christian congregations related to *their* handling of the Lord's Supper?

The Scots may be right in their "fencing" of the Holy Table, even to the point of making a physical symbol by the elders' standing between people and Table. The word was originally "defencing"—protecting the Table from profanation, and the people from the consequence of such an act.

If the consequences are so grave, we must seek the cause. Here this text speaks to us so simply, so unmistakably: "without discerning the Lord's body." To discern is much more than to understand, just as having insight is deeper than having sight. To discern is to recognize, to distinguish between this and other things. And more, to discern is to enter in some measure into what we see. An older generation liked to speak of a "man of discernment"—a man who could read behind another's eyes and words; a man more than sophisticated, more than merely wise; a man who seemed to comprehend another's mind and heart and purposes as if he had truly entered into the other's life.

Obviously, discerning the Lord's body is not a yes or no matter. There are surely degrees of discerning. For some who approach Christ in unbelief and distrust, the Table could only be an act of conscious irreverence. For some—such as children who have not come to the place where faith and understanding melt into commitment—the Table could only be an odd, unmeaning observance. For some who have only an "historical faith"—an acceptance that the Gospels may present facts about Jesus—the Table could on occasion be only very like a national Memorial Day.

All of us mingle insights with our imperfect vision. We discern in varying degrees of clarity. For us especially this word of warning is a voice of hope and encouragement, urging us to look afresh at this Table, entreating us to discern more clearly, more fully, more involvedly "the Lord's body."

This text does not mislead us. Its ambiguity is deliberate and purposed. Through all this section setting forth the institution of the Supper, Paul appears to try to make the statements that are at the same time briefest and most comprehensive. All the significance of the Supper is gathered into the fewest possible phrases. "The Lord's body" must certainly be the body of the cross.

Jesus ties cross to Table unmistakably by making it his last word to the disciples, "on the night when he was betrayed" (1 Cor. 11:23b). He might so easily have given the Supper weeks, months before. But he chose to make its connection with his passion unmistakable by giving it as close to the event of the cross as possible. "In remembrance . . ." he says, in the offering of the bread. "In remembrance . . ." he says, in the holding forth of the cup. Show forth his death, we are told. Announce—proclaim, it means.

It is his body of the cross, broken for us, which this Table sets before our eyes and faith. And all the benefits of his cross are offered for our participation. We know in this "body" ourselves taken up into his death. We sense its "for-us-ness." We discover again that "we are crucified with Christ"—yet we have life.

Dying *to* our sin are we, as he died *for* our sin. Living *unto* righteousness are we, as we are in him who died for us. In this body of his death we participate. Its blessings are given to us here. "Take, eat"—discern the body of his cross for you.

The Lord's body must be certainly more—it must be the body, his church.

The passage concerning the institution and the warning is embedded in Paul's long discussion of the Supper as observed wrongly in Corinth. They had debased the Table by keeping its forms, but keeping them in cliquishness and in self-interest. Their cardinal sin was the loss of fellowship, of mutual concern and service.

Paul had told them (1 Cor. 10:16) that the bread and cup "of blessing" were the "communion of the body and blood of the Lord"—the *koinonia*, the common possession. This was the way his hearers were accustomed to think of their citizenship, for example, as a "communion"—a commonly shared and valuable thing. It was just this they failed to discern at the Table. The body of Christ present at the Table was the body which his church is. In him we are all one body.

If ever we are to discover this, it is at the Table with the church. His covenant is to his people, and that covenant is clearly set forth to us together as a people again at this Table. Its reality is presented in a sign; its benefits are applied—sealed—to us.

We cannot come to the Table in preoccupation with ourselves, and in forgetfulness of our brethren. The life of mutual love we are enjoined to lead must come to expression here. And here above all other places we must discern the fountainhead of our oneness in him, the reason for our being members of each other.

We can fail to discern this body—the church—if we come seeking merely support for personal griefs and necessities. The fact that we are his body, the church, here forbids even individual preoccupation with our sins. We are *not* coming singly, but *as* his body. We take part in each other as we take part here in him; and as we participate in him we are made parts of each other.

"Take, eat . . ." In these signs you confirm your commitment to be of his body, the church. You will experience the reality of your being one with that innumerable company who have ceased to be single and alone and have found the joyous fellowship of the redeemed. Do you "discern" the church?

The Lord's body also must be the body of the ascended Lord. Jesus' word is not casual. "This *is* my body." It is the body of his redemptive work, the body of his church in the world, and it is the body of his present glorious lordship!

At this Table he offers not simply the benefits of his death and resurrection, but the very body in which he suffered, died, rose, and ascended to the right hand of his Father. Back into the presence of his Father, he took that body of his humiliation, now gloriously raised. This is the body of his present lordship—over the church and over all things. And *this* body we are to discern in the Table.

It takes no miracle to relate the bread and wine to him. He needs not to descend again to the Table, now at this place, again at that. But by the mighty working of his Spirit, he does truly give himself and his grace as ascended Lord of all of us here.

John Calvin so exactly understood this: "Allow him to remain in his heavenly glory. Raise your spirit and your heart thither that he may communicate himself to thee."

In his Geneva order for the Supper, Calvin insisted that the church remember this. He did not retain the empty formula of the *sursum corda;* but he insisted that the people fix their hearts in heavenly places, that they discern the ascended Lord who was truly present as he communicated himself to them.

But there is another way of discerning this same thing— his ascended lordship in the body of the Table.

The final words of the institution are determinative of all the rest: "until he come" (1 Cor. 11:26).

We can speak of his ascended lordship among us in terms of his coming now as surely some day he will come in the fullness of his might. You know the familiar German table prayer: "Come, Lord, sup with us." Thus the early liturgy of the church must have thought of his coming at the Table. These words were spoken in a dialogue between pastor and people: "If anyone be righteous, come; if he be guilty, repent." To which the people cried: "*Maranatha* (Come, Lord), Amen." This is your confident prayer: "*Maranatha. Lord, come!*"

This Table stands both as a moment in time and a moment in eternity. It was given for that time which lies between the close of the revelation recorded in scripture and the full revelation of his messianic coming. The Scriptures wait for him as they close with these words: "Come, Lord Jesus!" (Rev. 22:20b) This sacrament waits for him—in the glorious power of his lordship over us.

We would discern here the body of our ascended Lord.

Make now your prayer of faith and hope—and of great boldness: "*Maranatha.* Lord, come—now through this sacrament, as you surely will come—Lord of lords, King of kings."

Discern you *here* the Lord's body?

One Body, One Spirit

There is one body and one Spirit, just as you were called to the one hope that belongs to your call, one Lord, one faith, one baptism, one God and Father of us all.

—EPHESIANS 4:4-6a

☦ IN PAUL'S LETTER to the Ephesians he reaches the high concept of the unity of the church and lifts the challenge of "the unity of the Spirit in the bond of peace." "There is one body and one Spirit," he writes. Why then are there so many different, and differing churches in the world? Why so many divergences in doctrine and such sharp contradictions in practice among those who call themselves Christian?

Gradually but steadily it seems to be dawning on our churches that Jesus Christ cannot divide himself—that his own body, the church, must be one. The followers of Christ ought to be together. Some years ago leaders in overseas missionary work came face to face with the fact that our denominational differences have little meaning for new converts. They discovered that our many divisions into denom-

---

DR. REUBEN H. MUELLER, President of the Board of Bishops, The Evangelical United Brethren Church; chairman of the Division of Christian Education of the National Council of Churches of Christ

inational groups worked to confuse the Christian movement. The creation of the International Missionary Council was a strong effort to minimize these differences and to develop increasing areas of Christian cooperation. Through the leadership of Christian statesmen like John R. Mott and Archbishop William Temple, study and consultation conferences were organized in the areas of Christian Life and Work and Christian Faith and Order.

Eventually, under the impact of the tragedy of a worldwide war, the need became clear for a cooperative organization whereby the churches of Christ could come together in Christian unity and bring to the world Christ's healing and saving power. Amsterdam, Holland saw the launching in 1948 of the World Council of Churches. Into this fellowship were invited all Christian communions who confess "Jesus Christ as divine Lord and Savior." In the never-to-be-forgotten meeting in Amsterdam churchmen faced their differences but discovered that they were together in Jesus Christ, and therefore confidently heralded to all the world: "We intend to stay together." In their next world assembly at Evanston, Illinois in 1954 they reviewed the progress that had been made, evaluated their continuing problems, and announced just as confidently: "We intend to go forward together."

Thus the whole Christian world has been alerted to the movement toward Christian unity, but at the same time it has been made aware of the things that have divided Christ's followers in the past and often still create divisions today. It is important to realize that the frank facing of our differences is the first step to mutual understanding and appreciation. We are learning that unity does not necessarily mean conformity—not even uniformity.

At a conference on Faith and Order held in 1958 in Oberlin, Ohio—I was a delegate from our church—the main theme for consideration was "the nature of the unity that we seek in the church." It was most heartening to sense there that the major concern was with the "unity of the Spirit," more than with schemes of organic union. I suggest that the unity of the Spirit depends more upon our encounter with Jesus Christ and our relationship to him, than it does on our wisdom or achievements or positions. This is what our Master prayed about in his high priestly prayer in the upper room when he asked the Father "that they may all be one." It is what he made plain to his disciples when he instructed them about proper attitudes among his followers: "You have one teacher [Master], and you are all brethren" (Matt. 23:8b). To sharpen the meaning for ourselves we could well say, "Because Christ is our Master, *therefore* we are all brethren."

This fellowship depends not so much on who *we* are, or what we know or plan or achieve, as it depends upon who Jesus Christ is, and what our relationship is to him and to all that he came to do and is doing through his body—the church. We need to get our eyes off ourselves and on to him; off the fragmented expressions of his church found in our divisions, to his unified body; off our circumscribed understanding, to his revelation of the purposes of God. We need to learn that our doctrines, our human interpretations, are less important than the living truth which they try to imprison in creedal formulas.

"Christianity is not so much a body of doctrine as the living relationship between persons. God is not so much one about whom we are to think and philosophize as one with whom we have to do. True Christianity and true Christian faith move in living relationships." These are the words of Bishop Lesslie Newbigin of South India, writing about the unity that is in Jesus Christ, which is the real basis of our togetherness. He points up the basic relationship to God through Christ in the forgiveness of our sins and the acceptance into the fellowship of Christ. Thus the spiritual relationship and attitude is far more important than anything else, and the development of such a fellowship, graced by Christian charity, is our great need. In this fellowship the things that tend to separate us and keep us apart lose their power, and we are drawn to one another in Christ, by his Spirit. This, to me, is true Christian ecumenicity.

I know that this is all more easily stated than practiced or experienced. In theory, it may seem trite and worn by repetition, but whenever you dare to move from theory to practice you come face to face with a tremendously revolutionary principle for life. Let me try to apply this principle in the three chief tension areas of our times.

There is the area of race relations, in which tensions have been increasing all over the world. Everyone seems to have heard about America's concerns with the racial issue. In the winter of 1957, my wife and I went to Nigeria to visit our daughter and her family, who were in missionary service there. Among the first people to greet us upon our arrival was the native African manager of the United Africa Company. He was a keenly intelligent and capable businessman, entrusted with great responsibility for this inland trading post on the Benue River. After the formal greetings the first thing he said to me was, "Now tell me about Little Rock." And I told him. But I told him not only about the shame and disgrace of a state governor's action and about bigoted people who will sell out the education of their own children, but also about the white teenage Methodist high school student who stood up in a crowd of her fellow students and openly declared that it was not Christian to deny the colored youth an equal opportunity for an education with the white youth of her community.

One could tell about many of our communities in which

the members of a minority group have had their civil rights
and liberties protected and guaranteed. In this we in our
country are no different from the decent and good people
in many other lands who believe in the rights of man. Most
countries have their race problems and their minority
groups. But the fact is that only in those countries where the
Christian gospel has been proclaimed and has developed
ideals of righteousness and liberty, have men secured liberty
for themselves and their fellow men.

We will learn how to live together as brothers when we
have become the children of God through Jesus Christ.
Whenever our lives are changed and transformed by the
power of the redeeming, indwelling Christ, and become a
part of the life of his body, the church, there can be no race
distinctions to separate us and keep us apart from others.
Jesus Christ makes us one even across racial boundaries.

I maintain that in the area of relationships between
churches or communions, it is only the principle of "one
body, one Spirit" by which tensions can be resolved. I could
marshall dozens of illustrations from our many church groups
in the United States, and the sorry spectacle they set before
the world with their strife and competition. This, in the face
of the words of Jesus when he said, "I do not pray for these
only, but also for those who are to believe in me through
their word, that they may all be one; even as thou, Father, art
in me, and I in thee, that they also may be in us, so that the
world may believe that thou hast sent me" (John 17:20-21).
As I interpret this, the unity the church has in Christ is to
be the witness to the world that Jesus Christ is the Savior
sent by God.

But here again, the disparity between what the church is
and what the church is to be in Christ, is not confined to
our country. In the summer of 1958 I learned in Okinawa
that the representatives of dozens of denominational or-

ganizations are overrunning that island, and causing con-
sternation among the Okinawan Christians because of the
un-Christian competition and divisions among these "missionaries." And in Europe the relationships between many
churches is best described as a polite tolerance dictated by
the untoward circumstances of war times and postwar circumstances. Need I remind you how long it was true that
the established churches—their leadership, I mean—harried
and tried to suppress the free churches and similar movements; and in how many places the word "sect" is still pro-
nounced with a scornful curl of the lip!

And so, all over the world, the unbrotherly spirit manifested toward one another by many who call themselves followers of Jesus Christ is one of the greatest hindrances to the
progress of the gospel. One of our outstanding American
preachers, in a former generation, called this "the scandal of
modern Christianity." Of this we need to be cleansed. In my
judgment this can happen only through the Spirit of our
Lord Jesus Christ, bringing us into a unity of the spirit
that transcends the disunities of words and doctrines and
customs and prejudices and pride.

Often it seems that some of us are too much concerned
about "disputing about words to no purpose." I do not mean
that debate and discussion in matters of doctrine are unimportant. But it is possible to argue and debate about the
thirteen major theories of the atonement, for example, without ever having known for oneself the glorious experience of
at-one-ment with Jesus Christ through his redeeming grace.
To grant to others the right to sincerity in positions they
hold, even though we cannot subscribe wholly to those positions, seems to me to be part of that true spirit of Christlike-
ness that Paul wrote about to the Corinthians: "Now I know
in part" (1 Cor. 13:12b). To confess that at our best we
cannot imprison all the truth in our little human definitions,

and that others may have an understanding of certain facets of truth that we have not yet experienced, seems to me to be the only Christian way to consider one another's statements of belief. To recognize our honest differences and to learn to appreciate one another's contributions to the truth that is in Christ, seems to me to be of the spirit of Christ and a strong evidence of our unity in him. This spirit the Christian witness must recover if we are to have influence and power for God in the world. Thank God, there are some evidences in our time that this is slowly coming to pass.

I believe in the power of "one body, one Spirit" in the area of international relationships. The world is divided into two warring, scheming camps, East versus West. The western nations fear the Russian and Chinese coalition, with their satellite slave nations and their godless philosophies based on naked power. And the Soviet powers fear the West which has possessed ruling power in the world for a long time and has left some ugly blotches on the pages of history to prove how human, and sometimes how near the beast, they too are. Distrust and fear rules the relationships among the nations of the earth. Cold war and an uneasy peace haunt both our waking and our sleeping hours. Who of us, on either side, does not fear what a day may bring forth?

But when I think of all this, I come at last to remind myself that God's Word has promised that "the kingdom of the world has become the kingdom of our Lord and of his Christ, and he shall reign for ever and ever" (Rev. 11:15b). I believe that! For God has not abdicated his throne. Jesus Christ is still Savior and Lord and Prince of Peace! And he shall one day put all kingdoms under his feet, and reign as King of kings and Lord of lords, forever and ever.

The hope of the world is not in treaties made by statesmen who do not honor or fear God, and to whom the moral commandments are myth and legend, and whose word, therefore, cannot be trusted, even when signed with pomp and majesty in formal ceremonies. It is not in the piling up of atomic armaments that have within them the frankenstein power to annihilate civilization. It is not in the economic oppression of the underprivileged peoples by the more favored nations, even when the latter are motivated by paternalism. Our hope is in Christ, by whose indwelling spirit we come into oneness of spirit with him and thus with one another. This is the magnificent obsession of those who believe in Jesus Christ as Savior and Lord. And these are the true "peacemakers" whom Jesus called "blessed" and of whom he said that they would be known as "sons of God" (Matt. 5:9).

What chance will we ever have to bring this old world to enduring peace until professing, believing Christians leave their superstitions about politics and international relationships and begin to let the light of Jesus Christ shine into the dark places in the world? I am one who believes that it is beginning to shine in our times, through Christian men of influence and stature who are standing true to Christian ideals and are doing their utmost to preserve peace with honor. We pray for them daily. We preach hope even in this dark international hour. "For what we preach is not ourselves, but Jesus Christ as Lord, with ourselves as your servants for Jesus' sake. For it is the God who said, 'Let light shine out of darkness,' who has shone in our hearts to give the light of the knowledge of the glory of God in the face of Christ" (2 Cor. 4:5-6).

The Century of
Reconciliation

WHITTAKER CHAMBERS, once a key figure in the communist conspiracy as well as an editor of *Time* magazine and later a decisive factor in the conviction of Alger Hiss, recently wrote: "It is idle to talk about preventing the wreck of Western civilization. It is already a wreck from within. That is why we can hope to do little more now than to snatch a fingernail of a saint from the rack or a handful of ashes from the fagots and bury them secretly in a flowerpot against the day, ages hence, when a few men begin again to dare to believe that there was once something else, that something else is thinkable, and need some evidence of what it was, and the fortifying knowledge that there were those who, at the great nightfall, took loving thought to preserve the token of hope and truth."

This is a morbid summons to return to the caves, to make ready for "the great nightfall." We reject and repudiate the migraine message of the intellectual quitters whose cringing

DR. G. BROMLEY OXNAM, Bishop of The Methodist Church, the Washington Area; chairman of the Division of Christian Life and Work of the National Council of Churches

spirit is satisfied by burying a fingernail, a handful of ashes in a flowerpot. Has this ceased to be "our Father's world"? "Nothing can separate us from the love of God, which is in Christ Jesus." Has this promise been abrogated?

I should like to call the roll of recent centuries and then ask a question. The fifteenth century was the century of the Intellectual Revolution. The new learning emerged, the Renaissance; man experienced "the glory of the lighted mind." The sixteenth was the century of the Religious Revolution. The new learning with its intellectual honesty expressed itself in the Protestant Reformation, and man rejoiced in "the glory of the lighted soul." The seventeenth was the century of the Social Revolution, the seismic shock that brought to rubble a system that assumed kings ruled by divine right and that a society of nobles and of serfs was ordained of God and to question it was blasphemy. The eighteenth was the century of the Political Revolution, the American Revolution, the French Revolution, and the earlier English Revolution. Men talked of government of the people, by the people, and for the people; they held that government derives its just powers from the consent of the governed; that men were endowed by their Creator with certain "unalienable rights"; that men were created equal. Men learned that the state does not confer their liberties; it merely confirms them. They insisted these rights belong to us because we are men, because we are sons of God. We are endowed with them; they cannot be alienated. The nineteenth was the century of the Industrial Revolution, the coming of the steam-driven machine, the supersession of handicraft industry, the building of the factory system, the congestion into cities, the beginning of the capitalist era.

And the question? What is the twentieth century to be called? The "great nightfall"? The century of Collective

Homicide, resulting in world suicide? Is civilization to be cremated in the fires of a hydrogen blast? Call me naive, unrealistic, ingenuous—but I dare to affirm the belief that this will be called the century in which man abolished war, established economic justice, and realized racial brotherhood. It will be the century in which man learned how to live together, the century of the Great Reconciliation.

The first issue in the world struggle involves one's world view. If we would know a civilization we must ask three questions. How did they earn their living? How did they live together? How did they know their world? The first question, of course, has to do with economics; the second, with politics; and the third, with philosophy or religion. It is the third with which we are concerned. Our conduct is determined by our world view. Our faith determines what we live for and what we are willing to die for. The first issue in the world struggle, therefore, is the religious issue, the reconciliation of man and God. What is our faith?

Can we say with intellectual honesty, "I believe in God the Father Almighty"? Do we believe this is our Father's world, that the Eternal who keeps the stars in their courses notes the sparrow's fall? Do we hold that God's love is not an impersonal love for mankind in general but for you and me in particular, that man's relation to God is personal, direct, immediate? If we hold this, it follows that in all matters affecting our eternal welfare we are beyond the reach of any human dictator, we are not dependent upon any human institution. We can take anything that may happen to us in the certainty and the serenity that characterized Jesus. All of this is to say, as the theologian puts it, that God is relevant to all the activities of men.

The second of the crucial issues lies in the question: Can we reconcile the necessities of technology and the necessities of brotherhood? The answer is clear: We must. We must face the fact that there are necessities both in the realm of technology and of brotherhood.

It was Leon Trotsky in his volume *Toward Socialism or Capitalism* who insisted that the conflict between capitalism and communism would be determined by what he called "the relative coefficients of production." He meant that the system that produces goods the most efficiently will win. What he did not realize was that while man does need commodity, he likewise needs community. It is much more likely that the system that can develop community will survive when in competition with a system that produces commodity without community. It was Jesus who said that man does not live by bread alone.

We must work out a splendid synthesis wherein we may conserve the creative initiative that has flowed from individualism and appropriate the benefits that lie in collective endeavor. This means that while we keep the great advances of technology, maintain our research, manifest our organizing genius and all the rest of it, we do so in the presence of God.

It becomes apparent here that we must be guided less by fixed systems of economic dogma than by loyalty to ethical principle and the moral law. The American people, in their manifestation of the pioneering spirit and the democratic ideal, have wisely refused the strait jackets of economic dogma. I am one who believes that what we call free enterprise, in the overwhelming majority of our endeavor, will in the long run issue in greater creativity, result in larger productivity, and make a more fundamental contribution to freedom than any system that has yet evolved. This does not mean, however, that I will, on a doctrinaire basis, refuse other answers to particular problems that can better be met, let us say, by a collective approach.

Surely it is far better for us to have the highways of the nation collectively owned than to have a system of privately owned toll roads throughout the entire nation. I do not want anybody calling the American highway system socialist. I prefer to say it is American and it is good. We do provide for private education in the United States, and properly so, but I am proud of the fact that more than thirty million of our young people are in the schools and colleges of the public educational system. I do not want anybody calling that social-ist because it is collectively owned and democratically man-aged. I prefer to say it is American and it is good. I am sure also that the public corporation offers answers in certain areas that are better than private answers. Anyone who has really studied the Tennessee Valley Authority carefully knows that it is better to have a public corporation charged with developing all the resources of the valley in the unity with which nature endowed the valley than to have a private corporation there, no matter how efficient, developing power and light solely for the benefit of its stockholders. I do not want anybody coming in and telling me this is socialist. I prefer to say it is American and it is good.

In a word, we keep our minds free. We use the best an-swers to particular problems that we can find. The open mind now must be pledged to the moral law with its funda-mental test of measure lying in the questions: What does it do to personality? Does it express the law of love?

The third crucial issue involves the reconciliation of the interests of the one and the many. Here we deal with the agelong struggle between liberty and law, change and order. If we recall for a moment the psalmist's declaration, "I lift up my eyes to the hills," we might lift our eyes to the hills of ancient Greece. The political ideal of Greece was liberty. This is the principle of change. If we lift our eyes to the hills of Rome, we behold the political ideal which was law. This is the principle of order. But we know that liberty may lead to license, that law may move to tyranny; change may mean chaos, and order may become despotism. How do we reconcile liberty and law, change and order?

We who hold to the Christian view proudly summon the people to lift their eyes to another hill. It is outside the city of Jerusalem. It is crowned by a cross. Upon that hill we behold not a political ideal but the overwhelming, overmastering ideal of love. This is the principle of unity. When liberty and law are both subordinated to love, change becomes change in the interest of the person, and law is the law requisite to community. It is thus that the interests of the one and of the many are reconciled. It is thus that we lay hold upon those collective measures that do express the law of love.

The reconciliation of the interests of the one and of the many is not revolution, nor for that matter is it, first of all, reform; it is rather regeneration. This is a religious term, but it is a well-known term. It is a new spirit that is essential. It is the spirit that leaps artesian-like from love. Reconciliation is dependent upon regeneration and awaits the coming of the new man in Christ Jesus.

There is a fourth issue in the world struggle, namely, the reconciliation of the diversities of national cultures and the civilization of the world community. Just as the eventual reunion of the Christian community must be based upon the principle of diversity in unity, and all that has been discovered in the agelong search for God must be conserved for the benefit of the new Christian church, so, too, the cultural riches of the centuries now manifest in the nation-unit must be preserved for the benefit of the coming world community. All that has been achieved in the arts, the sciences, in philosophy and religion, by all the peoples of all time must become now the treasured heritage of all people in our time.

But this means peace, economic justice, racial brotherhood. It means the end of war and class struggle and the conflict of color. It means disarmament. It means law and order. The curse of conflict must pass. The cure of cooperation must come.

Peace has many aspects. I mention but three: the political, the economic, and the spiritual. There are three words that must be kept in mind when we consider the political aspects of peace: "cooperative," "continuous," and "consent." President Eisenhower has spoken of "cooperative peace." There can be no other. No nation can set up the conditions of peace; peace cannot be dictated. Coercion here is a contradiction in terms.

The second word is "continuous." The institutions of world law and order, like our own legislative assemblies and courts, our executive bodies, must be in continuous operation. So, too, the United Nations! Its agencies must be in continuous operation. It is now possible, under certain circumstances, to call even the Assembly to meet within twenty-four hours. We do not beat back disease at the world level except as public health officials, backed by the health forces of the nations, are continuously alert. Typhus knows no morality. It strikes, and must be struck immediately. Aggression occurs; a nation's independence is at stake. The forces of law must meet the henchmen of anarchy and at once. Illiteracy cannot be removed save by the continuous conduct of the educational process.

The third word is "consent." It is in a sense a corollary of cooperation. Cooperation is voluntary. But the fact of consent has wider significance. The structure and procedures of the world political organization must make it possible for all peoples to participate in the decisions of the world body and to vote upon the measures that are debated in the world forum, and that is what the Assembly of the United Nations is, a world forum. We cannot demand unanimity; that is to deny the democratic principle of majority rule. But we can give opportunity for all to be heard and for all to hear and for all to record conviction.

The second aspect of peace deals with economic considerations. Our own economy is involved in the economic aspects of peace. Communist control of vast markets heretofore open to us means a contracting world market. Expanding trade with the free world is essential. The tariff question becomes a spiritual issue. But here again we face the competition of commodities produced in areas with lower living standards. This means that free men elsewhere with machines and technicians can put commodities into the world market at a price we cannot meet because they pay less for labor. The answer is a rising standard of life for all men everywhere. What of our surpluses when the demands of war have passed? Are we not dependent upon increased consumption throughout the free world? This means that Point Four was not only idealism but practical realism, that the whole program of technical assistance is not merely an altruism that shortsighted isolationists condemn but sound self-interest that intelligent men understand. Economic problems have spiritual significance.

This brings us to the third aspect of peace, the spiritual. Mutual trust is essential to community. When we speak of peace we are thinking of world community. This means the extension of mutual respect and mutual trust to the world. Without mutual trust, legal arrangements, no matter how perfectly expressed in charters or constitutions, cannot function. Better to make progress in mutual trust, facing one problem after another, establishing one precedent after another, "line upon line, precept upon precept," than to confront differing nations in suspicion and in such an atmosphere seek to draft the ideal document. Charters that emerge from understanding are more likely to endure, since they express practice, than are charters composed of the compromises that represent as much unanimity as is possible under the conditions of disunity.

The world mission of Christianity with its revelation of the law of love revealed in a Person, with its insistence upon the infinite worth of the individual, with its test of greatness dependent upon service, with its final judgment, "as you did it to one of the least of these," is in fact the spiritual basis of peace. We need competent, convinced, consecrated laymen and laywomen who with the determination and the love that Jesus revealed in the Garden will kneel in commitment, saying, "Thy will be done" and with the same sense of mission will rise to face even a cross, if need be, that man may possess peace.

One
in Christ

✝ IN THE TWELFTH CHAPTER of his letter to the Corinthians, Paul exhorts them to union and harmony, and uses the comparison of a body to enforce his argument: You all have received different gifts and talents, yet there is no reason for disunion, just as there are different organs in the body yet there is no disunion. "A man's body is all one," he says, "though it has a number of different organs; and all this multitude of organs goes to make up one body; so it is with Christ. We too, all of us, have been baptized into a single body by the power of a single spirit, Jews and Greeks, slaves and free men alike; we have all been given to drink at a single source, the one Spirit." (See 1 Corinthians 12.)

Without doubt, sincere and thoughtful Christians everywhere, East and West, Protestant, Roman Catholic, and Eastern Orthodox, ardently long for the day when the unity of Christendom will become an accomplished fact. Toward this goal there is much striving and for it there is much prayer.

ARCHBISHOP-METROPOLITAN BOHDAN, Primate of the Ukrainian Orthodox Church of America (Jurisdiction of the Ecumenical Patriarchate)

142

It is possible that someone may say: "Yes, the comparison between a body and an association of men, made by Paul, is a happy one; each has his or her part to play, a different part, but each one's part contributes to the whole. One might imagine a worldly bishop of the eighteenth century using the illustration to exhort to tolerance of different views and a large-minded acceptance of diverse characteristics in the same organization of the church. The comparison is apt and thought provoking. But is there anything specifically religious about it? For that matter, is there anything specifically mystical about it? Further, in our day when the Christian world is torn with denominational conflicts, is there anything specially helpful about it in view of the divergence of opinions about the nature of the unity of the church? Is not the whole question of religious unity the question of how far individuals, groups, nations, may maintain their individuality and how far they should subordinate it to the common mind and the common action? The whole practical question is how far the metaphor of Paul may be pressed, and the metaphor itself offers no answer." So might some pessimists reason.

Is this passage from Paul merely a metaphor, or is it more? The Eastern Orthodox Church regards it as more, as indicating a reality beyond understanding, that can be expressed only by comparisons which fail of the reality, and yet give some idea of it. It would be a mistake to try to fit the reality of the unity of the church merely into this one figure of the body, helpful as it is. The same truth is affirmed by the figures of the vine and the branches, the sheepfold and the shepherd, the spouse and the beloved, by the figures of the kingdom, the heavenly city, the many mansions, the city built on a hill. Yet, the figure of the body seems peculiarly appropriate for several reasons:

First, the Eastern Orthodox ecclesiology is in essence

Christological. The body is a real and visible thing, not a shadow. The calling of the church "Christ's mystical body" affirms that it is an extension of the incarnational dispensation. Man is saved by visible means, not by purely spiritual ones. Human cooperation has its place in the divine dispensation just as does God's cooperation with man.

Second, the body is a living and growing organism, not a dead letter, not a code of laws. There are indeed laws of health to preserve the body, but they do not give life to the body; they cannot be violated with impunity, but they will not of themselves make the body live. Institutional religion and personal religion are united in the figure of the body.

Third, the body is composed of heterogeneous elements and organisms—so too must the church be. When Christ says, "Why do you persecute me?" (Acts 9:4b), he means it, for he lives in the members of his mystical body, the church. The love of Christ is stressed. Paul says, "It is unheard of that a man should bear ill will to his own flesh and blood; no, he keeps it fed and warmed; and so it is with Christ and his church; we are limbs of his body, flesh and bone we belong to him." (See Ephesians 5:29-30.) But this union does not destroy individuality or personality. On the contrary, it maintains it.

Fourth, the metaphor of the body stresses the unity of the church. Christ's prayer to the Father that those who believed in him might be one as Father and Son were one, takes on new meaning. Because Christ becomes one with us, therefore we share his relation to the Father, and the image of the Trinity becomes the image of the church. The Trinity asserts perfect unity without destruction of personality, asserts that God is charity, because the essence of God is to be three perfectly self-communicating Persons, each giving the whole of his nature and being. Therefore, and this we so often overlook, charity is the essence of the unity of the church. Charity or *agape* is the bond through which community and individuality meet.

To heal the wounds that have disfigured the mystical body, the church, it is necessary that Christians revive the bond of love among themselves and between man and God. Love motivated Christ to complete the redemption of man, to uplift him, and to bring him into union with God. In all his teachings, Christ emphasized love; in all his actions love was the cause, the means, the end. Both to friend and to foe was this powerful instrument employed. The apostles were instructed to use it in their mission. Love was the basic element in the kerygma. It has been the greatest and most powerful factor in the church from its beginning to the present. It is still the strongest force in the promotion of Christian unity.

We must face, however, the unhappy fact of the disunity of Christendom in our own day. It is not enough, in the promotion of unity, that we dream of the happy love feast in some apocalyptic future when all who follow Christ will sit down in harmony and complete oneness of mind. While we reject the hope of plenitude that can have no real basis except it be reserved for the end of the world, to become a reality after the parousia, we must identify the obstacles which stand in the way of the realization of this hope and formulate and take such positive steps as may be necessary to overcome these difficulties. What are the obstacles that keep Christians apart? What sets one part of the mystical body against the other?

It does not take great insight to identify as one of the divisive forces the emotion of fear. There is fear of losing autonomy and its supposed advantages. We persist in our desire to maintain our separateness, our isolation from the body of Christ. Union with others is sometimes imagined to be slavery or loss of individuality. Yet, true union should harmonize and improve each of the various complementary elements, leaving them their own personality and allowing them to pool their abilities for the one cause, the redeeming work of the Incarnate Word.

Another obstacle—a considerable one, but less difficult to deal with—is the mutual misunderstanding which time has hardened in the divided members of the church. People or groups of people whose relations have long been broken accumulate prejudices which breed a natural aversion for making contact again. By living apart they become accustomed to doing without each other and imagine themselves sufficient to themselves in an enclosed sphere. This is of course contrary to the essential principle of the hierarchical church of Christ, where every member is vivified by the others and all form that communion of saints in which each is enriched by the merits and actions of all, sharing in a common spiritual life which comes from the Holy Spirit.

Lack of understanding among Christians is also increased by more or less important differences in modes of thought and ways of life. If we are to understand each other we must not be content with speaking the same language, we must shape ourselves to the mentality and traditions of others and be ready, should the cause need it, to emerge from our own mentality and ideas and enter those of others.

This is the only way toward understanding and knowing one another. Christian agape joined to this knowledge can smooth out many difficulties which prevent approach and agreement among Protestants, Roman Catholics, and Eastern Orthodox Christians. Approach, understanding, mutual sympathy among separated Christians must be encouraged by contact in the sphere of ordinary human relations, not simply in the area of theological discussions. We must use all we can offer to draw others to us and meet them where they are. We need to develop the habit of mutual intercourse.

The church was born under the sign of charity, and she must always appear clothed in charity.

Doctrinal agreement among separated Christians will not be easy to achieve, even in the bond of mutual love, but it is essential if there is to be unity. Such agreement, in the context of an effort to bring professing Christians into unity, must begin with the doctrine of the church, with ecclesiology. Until Christians can agree in their definition of the church, it is impossible for all to strive to participate in its true unity. At present the church is variously defined as an organism; the mystical body of Christ; an organization, divinely instituted; a divine society; the invisible company of the faithful throughout the world; a voluntary organization of believers; a disrupted entity, consisting of bodies which possess a creed, a ministry, sacraments, and the like; the spiritual department of the State. These definitions, though not all mutually exclusive, exhibit such fundamental oppositions and contradictions that unity becomes a mere will-o'-the-wisp until they are resolved into one. The unity of an organism is of a very different character from the unity of the invisible company of the faithful and that of a voluntary organization of believers; very different from that of a divine society.

The Eastern Orthodox Catholic conception of church unity implies, as the Orthodox delegates at the Second Assembly of the World Council of Churches meeting at Evanston in 1954 asserted, that the "whole of the Christian faith should be regarded as one indivisible unity. It is not enough to accept just certain particular doctrines, basic as they may be in themselves, for example, that Christ is God and Savior. It is compelling that all doctrines as formulated by the Seven Ecumenical Councils, as well as the totality of the teaching of the early, undivided church, should be accepted. . . . From the Orthodox viewpoint, reunion of Christendom can be

achieved solely on the basis of the total, dogmatic faith of
the early, undivided church without either subtraction or
alteration. . . . Thus, when we are considering the problem
of church unity, we cannot envisage it in any other way than
as the complete restoration of the total faith and the total
episcopal structure of the church which is basic to the sacramental life of the church."

The Orthodox Church calls herself the One, Holy, Orthodox, Catholic, and Apostolic Church and affirms that she
alone has preserved in full and intact "the faith once delivered unto the saints." It is not in a spirit of human pride
that this belief is so firmly held by Orthodoxy, nor does this
affirmation reflect a lack of charity toward Christians of other
denominations. With profound and humble gratitude the
Orthodox Church looks to the Holy Spirit as the Guardian
and Preserver of this faith which has been preserved complete within her. Yet she longs for the day when there may
be a sharing of this faith and practice in mutual love and
unity with all who have been baptized into Christ.

Our happiness and joy in the holy faith cannot be constant, complete, surpassing expectation, and brimming over,
like that which our Lord promises us in John; we see the
Christian world torn apart too much by dissension though
using the name of the same Father and the same Elder Brother, and possessing a heritage which springs from a common
Source. Our joy cannot be full as long as these discords ef-
fectively prevent us from finding all mankind united within
the mystical body of Christ.

The nails of the cross hold stretched open for all human
time the hands of the Lord Jesus Christ to gather together
a rebellious, wayward people. More powerful and more un-
yielding than the nails, sweeter and more soothing to his
agony and torture, may our hands, raised in prayer, support
and strengthen—if one may be permitted the comparison,

like the hands of Hur and Aaron—the prayer of the Last Supper and the Lord's sacrifice on Calvary, that, in accordance with the earnest desire of the Savior, he may gather together in his mystical body all his scattered children for whom he shed his blood. These children all took to his cross, but today they are still divided among themselves, strangers in part to one another, almost like hostile brothers grouped around the bed of a father or mother whom each loves sincerely but in his own way. May the Lord incline his head, close his arms, and gather beneath the same mantle of his blood all his children without exception, to be infinitely loved, to be one in mind and heart and purpose.

What Is a Church?

✝ NO ISSUE IS MORE widely discussed among Christians in
our time than the one usually referred to as "the doctrine of the church." It is the one on which church officials
and professional theologians generally get bogged down; and
this is probably due in the main to the fact that when they
sit down at conference tables together each labors under a
subconscious sense of responsibility to defend the traditions
which he represents and to advocate those traditions as being
a little truer to the New Testament beginnings and a little
more certain to preserve the church as it ought to be preserved.

Yet, strangely enough, when the average pastor of almost
any denomination preaches to his people on this subject he
is likely—whether Congregationalist or Episcopalian or Presbyterian or Lutheran or some other—to say pretty much
the same thing. In the setting of a congregation at worship
his utterance tends to be more affirmative of commonly felt
truth and less defensive and argumentative in the interests
of one tradition as against another.

What is a church? I venture here an approach to the answer; and I do so with some confidence that the substance of

DR. JAMES E. WAGNER, President of the Evangelical and
Reformed Church; Co-president of the United Church of Christ

150

this answer would be likely to elicit an appreciative Amen from almost any Christian congregation of whatever denomination. I will ask you to have in mind two passages of New Testament scripture. One of them is the familiar assurance of our Lord: "Where two or three are gathered in my name, there am I in the midst of them" (Matt. 18:20). The other is less familiar, highly figurative in its language, and in the King James Version of the Bible reads: "Ye are come unto mount Sion, and unto the city of the living God, the heavenly Jerusalem, and to an innumerable company of angels, to the general assembly and church of the firstborn, which are written in heaven" (Heb. 12:22-23a).

I shall say little further directly about these two passages. I point out only that, whatever else they may mean, taken together they suggest that if you want the full answer to the question, What is a church? your thought and imagination must take in the wide sweep which ranges from the little gathering of two or three or ten or twelve who have little else in common except that they love the Lord Jesus and seek to do his will—that is the church local and in miniature —to that mystic fellowship which overflows the boundaries of time and space and of which the outsider, the unbeliever, can know nothing, "the innumerable host of the redeemed of all ages who have lived and died in the Lord and now live with him for evermore."

Now, for an answer to a question which really asks for the definition of a word, a good place to begin is with the dictionary; and you will find that the dictionary recognizes at least four uses of the word church. In its most comprehensive sense, as in the phrase "the Christian church," the word is used to distinguish all the followers of Christ throughout the world from the followers of Buddha or Confucius or Muhammad or any of the founders of the great ethnic religions. There are rich connotations to the word church when it is used in this way; for it is a reminder that, however much our traditions have differed in the past, however much we differ or seem to differ from each other in the present, all of us— Protestant, Roman Catholic, Eastern Orthodox—stand on common ground.

All of us bear Christ's name. All of us call him Lord and Savior. All of us profess to seek his kingdom. And all of us are being driven by the persistent gnawing of secularism and materialism at the vitals of all faith, by the aggressive resurgence of the non-Christian religions offering increasing competition with missionary zeal, and by the pressures of atheistic communism pushing its claims with an evangelistic passion which puts to shame our casual devotion—by forces such as these all of us are being driven to recognize that we must all stand together or all together fall.

It is not only the compulsion of exterior events, however, that is giving us a fresh sense of our oneness in Christ. The ecumenical movement, as in the National and World Councils of Churches, has encouraged men and women of many denominations, Protestants and Eastern Orthodox, to talk and worship and work together with the result of a glad realization that beneath their differences they hold in common a core of Christian faith and devotion. Indeed, it is not unknown in our day for Protestants and Roman Catholics to sit down with one another to explore their differences and also those areas in which they stand together. The word church in this most comprehensive usage is really bringing us closer to each other and thus enriching for us the meaning of the word.

A second but somewhat more limited use of the word church which the dictionary recognizes is when it is virtually synonymous with denomination. Thus we speak of the Methodist Church, the United Lutheran Church, the United Presbyterian Church, the United Church of Christ, the Evangelical and Reformed Church, the United Church of Canada, and so on. Incidentally, neither Christians nor those outside the church should minimize the significance of the way, increasingly over the past forty years, the word united has been incorporated into denominational names. Something more than ordinary has been happening among once-divided Christian communions.

We have begun to outlive the earlier competitiveness, and to rise above a sectarianism in which each Christian communion practically disavowed other Christian communions as being not quite Christian. But as the fresh realization of our oneness in Christ has grown, a peculiar thing has been happening which at first glance seemed to deny that growth; for, as denominations worked more and more with each other and as some actually began to think of uniting, they found themselves giving more attention to their own distinctive origins and doctrinal viewpoints and thus developing a new denominational self-consciousness. At first this development was feared as likely to undercut the ecumenical movement.

What is now becoming clear is that, instead, this was one way by which each denomination, as it entered more deeply into cooperation with and appreciation of other denominations, brought to that widening, deepening fellowship a fuller contribution of its own understanding and practice of the Christian faith. At the very moment when Christians are rising above denominationalism they are acquiring a new appreciation of what it meant in Christian history, and the word church in this sense adds to the answer to the question, What is a church?

A third dictionary definition of the word church is that it designates a sacred building set apart and dedicated to the worship and service of the God and Father of our Lord Jesus Christ. Some such definition would be needed to distinguish it from a Jewish synagogue, a Muslim mosque, a Buddhist temple, or the sacred building of any of the other great faiths. This, too, is a rich and abundant connotation of what a church is. It is more than the architectural form which marks it off from other public buildings, more than the stone and brick and wood and steel, the stained glass windows, the pews, and other furnishings. It is what goes on within such a building that really makes it a church. Within its walls are enshrined the highest, holiest memories of a people's life. Here they bring their little children to be consecrated to God in the sacrament of Christian baptism. Here a few years later those children come to assume in their confirmation vows or other public profession of faith the responsibilities and the hopes which their parents assumed in their behalf when as infants they were baptized. Here, not many years later, those same children now grown to young manhood and womanhood stand for the wedding ceremony in order that upon their marriage may be invoked the sanctions and blessings of Eternity. And to the church once again we turn when it becomes our lot to lay our beloved dead away, that above the otherwise black and empty countenance of death may be raised the halo of that hope which derives from the promises of God's Holy Word. It is literally true that from cradle to grave, and in all the varying joys and sorrows which come between, the great moments of our lives center in that building which is "our church."

And that leads readily to the dictionary's fourth definition of a church—not the building but the congregation of people that regularly gather within its walls. The distinction is reflected in two of the colloquialisms of our common speech. When you say, "I'm going up to church," you are likely to be talking about the building located on a specific corner in your town or on a hilltop or at a crossroads out in the countryside. But when you say, "I belong to such-and-such church," you are obviously referring, not to a building, but to the company of friendly and familiar faces with whom it is your habit to gather Sunday after Sunday for the worship of God and for fellowship and study with those who, like yourself, are followers of Christ.

"A church," one of my teachers, the late Theodore F. Herman, used to say, "is a *con*gregation, not an *ag*gregation." A handful of marbles is an aggregation, with no relationship to each other except that of proximity. But a *con*gregation, ah! that is something else. That is a local fellowship of followers of Christ who, as the old hymn has it, "share our mutual woes, our mutual burdens bear; and often for each other flows the sympathizing tear." They are so close to each other, and become even closer as the years go by and the sum of joys and sorrows, hopes and fears and yearnings they have shared continues to multiply.

Their very closeness to each other is a source of strength. For, as the lovely allegory in 1 Corinthians 12 expresses it, "If one member suffers, all suffer together; if one member is honored, all rejoice together" (1 Cor. 12:26). And, it should be noted, the intimacy which makes the congregation a source of strength can be also a major hazard of the Christian life. We are so close together that we know each other well, perhaps too well! We tend to take each other for granted. We know each other's faults and weaknesses so well that, unless we are careful and are possessed of a sense of humor, the faults and weaknesses may blind us to the spiritual power and nobility of each other.

The Screwtape Letters, one of the earlier books of that English Christian layman and scholar, C. S. Lewis, addresses itself to this peril. The book is made up of what purports to be a series of letters written by the prince of devils to his nephew, an imp who has been sent to earth on a special assignment. That assignment is, not to tempt sinners and un-

believers into worse sin and unbelief, but to woo Christians
away from Christ and the church. Now, my dear nephew,
the uncle prince of devils writes in effect in one of the first
of these letters, if you approach your "prospect" with any
such argument as that it is unreasonable, illogical, to be a
follower of Christ, you will get nowhere with him. But if
you can whisper in his ear that the soprano is singing off key
in the anthem, or the usher's shoes squeak as he moves up
and down the aisle, or the minister's hair is parted as no self-
respecting minister should part his hair, and get your prospect irritated and annoyed at some little human fact like
this in the church to which he belongs, you will have taken
the first successful step toward alienating this Christian from
Christ and the church.

Despite the perennial peril of congregational life in all
its intimacy, it is right there in the intimacy of congregational
life, where the two or three or the two or three hundred
share so deeply with each other, that the miracle and wonder
of the meaning of church comes to the full. It is an assembly
and fellowship of the people of God, whose life centers in
One whom they call Lord, and who know that "here we have
no lasting city, but we seek the city which is to come . . . the
city which has foundations, whose builder and maker is
God" (Heb. 13:14; 11:10b), a people who lean the more
heavily on each other the more clearly they become aware
that their life on earth is a pilgrimage and their destiny lies
beyond earth and time.

The whole of Christendom, the denomination which has
cradled and nurtured our spiritual life, the "house of God"
to which we go, the congregation to which we belong, to all
of this, to each of these, the dictionary would point in answer to the question, What is a church? The church is all
that the dictionary hints at. But it is more, infinitely more;
and if all one knows about the church is what the dictionary

tells him, if he never gets to know the church "from the inside" by sharing its life and work, he misses the thrill and splendor of what the church and belonging to it really mean. For within its fellowship, and only within its fellowship, he will learn three things about the church of which the dictionary cannot possibly speak.

He will learn that *the church is a fellowship which reaches farther back* than man's mind and imagination can carry him into his own past history. It is a fellowship which, in unbroken succession, goes back to Christ himself, to the apostles and martyrs, and back of them through the Old Testament line to the prophets and Moses and Abraham, back indeed to that dim far-off beginning when "the first man stood God-conquered with his face to heaven upturned." A member of Christ's church belongs to that kind of ageless fellowship.

He will learn that *the church is a fellowship which reaches out* "to the uttermost parts of the earth." It includes the army of missionaries on distant continents and the isles of the sea, and their converts, the younger churches in what used to be known as "heathen lands," and the rising tide of devout and able native Christian leaders in Asia and Africa and Latin America and the Pacific Islands. The truly worldwide extent of this fellowship is reflected in the report that at least some portion of the Bible—one of the Gospels, the book of Psalms, the New Testament, in many instances the whole Bible—has now been translated into approximately 1,200 languages and dialects each of which is spoken somewhere on this earth; and the translations have been made only because in faraway places where those languages are spoken the Cross has been planted and other "two's and three's" have been gathered together in Christ's name. And the fellowship reaches out, not only geographically, but to all the world's wandering and distressed—the downtrodden, the poor, the rich, the powerful, the learned, the ignorant—

and gathers them into its widening embrace, doing so in a Christian appropriation of an ancient pagan's phrase to insist that "nothing human is foreign to God or beyond his love and care."

And finally, the inquirer who moves beyond the dictionary will learn that the church is a fellowship which not only reaches back and reaches out, but also *reaches up until it moves out of time into eternity.* This is probably the truth about the church which the unbelieving outsider will have most difficulty in understanding, indeed will find it impossible to understand. But it is what the church in faith affirms about itself when it recites the Apostles' Creed with its phrases "holy Catholic Church; the communion of saints." This is what a congregation will think of when it hears reference to "the great cloud of witnesses looking down upon us from the heavenly world." This is what the fathers had in mind when they spoke of the church militant and the church triumphant, picturing the latter as composed of those whom, in Cardinal Newman's phrase, "we've loved long since, and lost awhile." This is what the church believes and from which it derives its ultimate comfort and hope when it reads from Paul, "For we know that if the earthly tent we live in is destroyed, we have a building from God, a house not made with hands, eternal in the heavens" (2 Cor. 5:1).

For an adequate answer to the question, What is a church? one must take the best words which the dictionary affords, and add to them the visions of all earth's poets and prophets and dreamers, and something of the infinitude of space and history and of time which loses itself in eternity; and one will then only have begun to sense that what begins at a mourners' bench or at the chancel rail where confirmands kneel to make their vows, introduces the believing heart to a fellowship which is beyond all describing—the church of the living God.

The Great Right Way

And when the prophet who had brought him back from the way heard of it, he said, "It is the man of God, who disobeyed the word of the Lord; therefore the Lord has given him to the lion, which has torn him and slain him, according to the word which the Lord spoke to him."

—I KINGS 13:26

THE BIRTH OF THE GREAT religion of the Holy Spirit in the ancient world is associated with Abraham. His children never quite solved the problem of abandoning the old gods for the real God. The strange old Bible classic of our text pictures one of the many instances of their infidelity.

A man of God is sent from Judah to Israel to condemn the blasphemy of the idolatrous and profligate king, Jeroboam, who for political purposes is desecrating the altar at Bethel by doing sacrifice to the bulls of Egypt. God verifies his message when he pronounces a curse upon the altar, restrains the king with paralysis when he seeks to kill the man of God, restores him when he appeals for mercy.

Remembering that he is under the command of God not to socialize in any way, as by breaking bread or drinking water with these traitors and idolators, the man of God re-

DR. WILLIAM JACOB WALLS, Senior Bishop of the African Methodist Episcopal Zion Church

fuses the king's hospitality. But an old prophet, himself a collaborator with Jeroboam's idolatry, deceives him and persuades him to break his compact with God and go home with him for festivity. Later, on his way back to Judah the man of God is killed by a lion. His violent death is interpreted as punishment for his disobedience to God.

The man of God was tired, hungry, and lonesome. This affected his conviction and his power to resist the lying old prophet. With his loss of conviction came a weakening of the spirit of sacrifice. The sensuous appetites were in conflict with his duty.

A man's philosophy of life grows out of desires, controlled or uncontrolled: "To set the mind on the flesh is death, but to set the mind on the Spirit is life and peace" (Rom. 8:6). From the temptation of the first pair in Eden to Jesus in the wilderness the struggle was between the intangibles and the tangibles, between vision and appetite. "You seek me, not because you saw signs, but because you ate your fill of the loaves" (John 6:26b), Jesus said to the multitude who had crossed the sea searching for him. "I pommel my body," said Paul, "and subdue it, lest after preaching to others I myself should be disqualified" (1 Cor. 9:27). So Paul found, as we all may, enduring courage for God's way. He who has never denied himself of some necessity for a higher good has never truly lived.

Up to a point the man of God from Judah had successfully carried out his mission. He had been under great tension in facing the profligate king, but the battle of wits and spirit had been won by him. Now he had that dangerous thing, leisure, and was faced with new choice. (Satan comes most easily when we are relaxed in success.) He had won his cause but he had not mastered himself. God had given him the privilege of being his messenger, but he belied his mission and let God down. He must die to vindicate God's meaning in Israel and save his prophecy. This is the common weakness: preaching truth but failing to live truthfully. As Shakespeare wrote: "If to do were as easy as to know what 'twere good to do, chapels had been churches and poor men's cottages, princes' palaces."

The man of God was a member of the true church sent by God to rebuke sin, but he made the mistake of accepting the friendship of enemies of the church. He became chummy with the lying prophet and his friends, charmed by sophisticated words. The church is still the primary association of those who believe and live the way of Christ, but in our time we have made it hard in the church to find God's way. The church is too often filled with compromisers of God's standards. Too much we have excused ourselves from the fundamentals of divine teaching and bypassed Christian mandates with weasel words.

There appears to be "no harm" in anything men want to do these days, and the church is choked with people who live licentiously, practice hatred of class and race and nation, and despise the standards of personal and group living of our great faith. Hence the good life is retarded, evil stalks at large and corrupts our Christian democracy, scandals infest areas of education, politics, business, social relations, amusements, public relations, and mediums of communication. Labor and industry grow equally unjust and corrupt with greed. Even the church itself is held back from asserting the essence of its mission to make the Christian community a family of brotherly love and speed the world toward peace and good will, all of which God promised through Jesus.

We are wont to say that God is responsible for men's status and should keep them from evil, but we know we are slandering God when we say it. God could not make man a free human being and deny the right of choice simultaneously. When a man fails, he places the blame on God. Usually, when one succeeds, he says, "I am a self-made man." The truth is that God has indeed limited himself in his partnership with us, but we are free only to make choices, subject to divine sovereignty. When we leave God out, we sign our own doom. Our guide is a conscience enlightened in righteousness.

Soon after the last world war, a national congress was assembled in the old Coliseum in Chicago. I was asked to dismiss a session with prayer. I found the meeting honeycombed with communism and atheism. After a well-known poet read a poem with the words, "Now we know God does not care," and others made speeches along that line, I left the platform. They were making an excursion away from God and I did not feel that they should be aided with a benediction. A young woman with a Master's degree questioned my position. She blurted out, "How far have we gotten, going with God?" I reminded her of Lincoln's Emancipation Proclamation and its blood cost, and the sacrifices made by abolitionists and Christian missionaries for the freedom and culture of the Negro.

Later, I went into Russia. I returned more deeply convinced that when people do not serve the God who created them, they create a god to serve themselves. "Can man make for himself gods? Such are no gods!" (Jer. 16:20)

As men believe their god to be, they themselves become. The old rival gods with the vices of their human creators, kept their devotees forever at war and in confusion by jealousies and hatred, atomism and racism. As today, men kept asking, "Where is the good way, that we may walk therein?"

In that black and dark night, Abraham raised the new concept by the inquiry: "Shall not the Judge of all the earth do right?" (Gen. 18:25b) And he started the world on the quest of the one God whose character is righteousness. On the very spot where Abraham had raised his altar to a just and merciful God at Luz, renamed Bethel by Jacob after his dream there, Jeroboam was committing the sin of calf worship which would scatter the ten tribes to the four winds, because they had lost God the only unifier.

Lincoln, like Abraham, trusted in the divine power and righteousness. A minister during the war anxiously urged a more resolute policy on slavery: "If we do not do right I believe God will let us go to our own ruin. But if we do right he will lead us safely and crown our arms with victory." Lincoln replied: "My faith is greater than yours. But I also believe God will compel us to do right in order that he may do these things, not so much because we desire them as that they accord with his plans of dealing with this nation, in the midst of which he means to establish justice. . . . I have felt his hand upon me in great trials and submitted to his guidance, and I trust that as he shall further open the way, I will be ready to walk therein, relying on his help and trusting in his goodness and wisdom."

God has given our America a mission. This thought is pointed up strongly by the philosopher William Ernest Hocking in his lecture on "Evangelism": "The condition of the world is the obligation of the church, and that means the whole world. . . . For the moment we (of America and Europe) begin to think of Christianity as a special cult of our own we have ceased to be Christians."

We must, as our Lord commanded, continue to carry the gospel to all men everywhere, respecting the social and spiritual good of all cultures. If we turn back to self-loving and racial and national spurning of other people and their revelations as heathen only, we will lose Christianity.

Lincoln's words "This nation under God" were taken as the motto of the uniting conference of our National Council of Churches. Our national leaders may visit, as our President and representatives do, in non-Christian lands, seeking good will and understanding. But we must not compromise our mission and endorse pagan customs. We must guard against becoming chummy with non-Christian peoples and practicing their ways, remembering that we are ambassadors of Christ, and of the almighty God of Israel, lest we be lost and lose the world we are called to save.

The power to stay through with God comes from above. But we must tarry with him to receive that power. He is never far from us. Faith is human weakness transformed into divine strength. It is finding the will of God in one's self. The kingdom of God is in us. The human self moves through surrender into God's will and the unpredictable growth begins, from depths resident in man into God's depths from whom man came. Here, something new is born from energies flowing through human experience from the greatest being in the universe.

We recognize this new creation by saintly names. Sometimes we call it by such names as John, Paul, Polycarp, St. Francis, St. Cecilia, St. Sebastian, John Huss, Luther, Wesley, Ghandi, Livingstone, Schweitzer, Lincoln, Fanny Crosby, Francis Willard, Frederick Douglass, Harriet Tubman.

God's creativity is ever coming into our world. Our summons is to find the will of God in our life and follow it through. This is the ultimate base of all religion. It is the depths of God and man's depths moving into each other, producing the greatest miracle of the ages—mankind united for all good. America was committed to the search for God's will by our forefathers. The church, with her call for equality in the good life for all humans, has the peril of being based on the intangible. It runs the risk of being lost in the self-pleasing struggles of power groups. But by this universal depth the nation stands or falls.

We constantly hear, in our struggle for justice and love in all human relations, the cry: "This is not the time—do not try to carry us too fast." But in the pressure of this atomic age, justice and love cannot wait. Men of God are called to go about God's business with urgency, letting nothing turn them from the great right way.

His Way and Ours

For my thoughts are not your thoughts, neither are your
ways my ways, says the Lord. —ISAIAH 55:8

✝ "WHY SHOULD GOD let such a thing happen?" This and
similar anguished cries are often on the lips of even
devout Christians. So much of what happens in this world
seems unjust and almost capricious. It is not hard to understand agnosticism. How can we believe in a good and loving
God when we see and experience so many cruel and painful
things? The dilemma appears at many levels in Christian
experience. We meet it in prayer: the child who prays for
a new toy, the woman who prays for the life of her beloved,
the saint who prays for the peace of the world. More often
than not, that for which we pray is denied. How can God do
this, when we have been good, and have tried to follow his
laws?

Or, on another level, we see the wicked and the selfish
flourishing and good and gentle people suffering or deprived.
Where is the justice in this? We fashion a church as we
feel sure God wants it. Our doctrine and order and worship are completely orthodox. And we see, to our chagrin,

DR. CYNTHIA C. WEDEL, member of the National Council
of the Protestant Episcopal Church; chairman of the Broadcast-
ing and Film Commission of the National Council of Churches

166

that a quite unorthodox group who call themselves Christians are rewarded with far greater success than we. Or, in obedience to what we feel sure is the will of God, we go to war, only to find that our enemy is also fighting to do God's will!

What can the Christian say, to himself or to others, when such problems arise? Throughout human history, men have struggled with these questions. Some have found belief in God impossible. Others have been content to accept on the authority of someone else that there is a loving and powerful God, in spite of evidence to the contrary, and have stifled any question or rebellion. But for many of us, especially in an age of questioning and skepticism, it seems important to try to find an answer to the dilemma. A complete answer is, of course, far beyond the scope of a brief meditation, but it is worth while to seek even partial answers.

May a clue be found, perhaps, by going back to the story of creation? The writers of the early chapters of Genesis had amazing insight into the ways of God with man, and man's response to his creator. Whatever adjustments our knowledge of geology or biology may force us to make in our interpretation of these biblical accounts, we cannot deny that they are profoundly true of human nature as we all know and experience it. Probably the most telling phrase in the whole story is that God made man "in his own image." The writer is saying that God deliberately created man as a "little god," endowed with some degree of the qualities of his creator. Only in his mortality did he differ radically.

As a result of his godlikeness, man was quick to set himself up as his own god—defying his creator, obeying his own will, seeking to run the world in his own way. In the Genesis story we can see clearly that God's plan for his universe and for man was benevolent. If man could, voluntarily, have surrendered his pride and self-will and been obedient to God, quite possibly sin and selfishness, pain and sorrow need never have come into human experience. But man could not resist trying out his godlike qualities and his ability to say no to God. And apparently it was God's plan from the beginning not to coerce man, but to let him be free.

An evidence of our human tendency to be our own gods is the way in which we establish standards of right and wrong, good and bad, justice and injustice, and assume that *our* standards are God's standards. It is our constant temptation to try to reverse the creation story and to make God over in our image. Our ideas of love, or of good, or even of right and wrong, have been developed out of our own experience. Because we find it difficult, if not impossible, to love someone who is quite unlovable, and because we have found that to win human love we usually seem to have to earn it by good works or obedience or virtue, we imagine that God's love must be like ours. The history of religion is largely a history of man's striving, by way of sacrifice, or ritual, or moral goodness, to win the favor and love of God. The basic good news of Christianity is that this is not God's way. "While we were yet sinners Christ died for us" (Rom. 5:8b) —an amazing statement of Paul! The Christian faith proclaims that God loves us simply because he is God and we are his children, that he came and lived among us and died on a cross to make this clear to us. But most of the time we find ourselves saying, "It can't really be true. No one acts that way." We continue to try to make God in our own image!

Another illustration of our inability to accept God's ways can be found in our feelings and attitudes about death. Indeed, it is frequently in connection with death that we are tempted to express our greatest rebellion and sense of injustice. I remember, some years ago, being in a group of devoted church people. We were shocked to learn of the serious illness of a young woman known to most of us. She was dying of cancer and leaving three young children. We prayed for her and her family. The difficult question, "Why should this happen?" was always present. Then one member of the group said, "Isn't it strange how we Christians, like everyone else, assume that death is a bad thing? Why do we take it for granted that death is the worst possible event?" The question startled all of us, for we had, indeed, been doing just that. From the human point of view, of course, death is bad. It is so completely final. When we lose one we love, we are lonely and bereaved. But is our human point of view the only one, or the right one?

There would seem to be only two possible answers to the pain and injustice of the world, and to the finality of death. Either there is no God, and human life is a meaningless and tragic accident of the evolutionary process, or the God of the Bible is real but "his ways are not our ways." There is no other choice. People have accepted the first alternative and lived by it. But for many of us this is impossible for it leaves too many things unexplained. Whence our ideas of God? Whence our conscience, and our sense of ultimate right and wrong? How explain the intricacies and lawfulness of the universe without intelligence behind it? What is the source of the strength and peace which saints both great and small have found even in the midst of human tragedy? Whence even our questioning of God?

These and many other mysteries have driven men to a belief in God. In the Christian church we have held that the nature of God is disclosed to us in the Bible, and supremely in Jesus Christ. But, having said that, we usually proceed to behave as though much of what the Bible or our Lord have told us is not true. Our text is an example. Isaiah quotes the Lord God as saying, "My thoughts are not your thoughts, neither are your ways my ways." Yet we continue to expect God to run his universe according to our expectations. This explains in part the many paradoxes of the Christian faith. Most of these paradoxes are the confronting of our usual human way of behaving with God's different way. "He who would save his life must lose it." (See Matthew 10:39.) "He who would be greatest among you, let him be your servant." (See Mark 10:43.) We may assent to these ideas, yet even in our churches we are anxious about preserving our lives—the life of our own group, our own way of doing things. Even among Christians there is much "status seeking," and all too little eagerness to serve.

In the Sermon on the Mount, our Lord seems to be trying to make explicit what God's ways are, and how he wants us to behave. It may be well to consider some of these "hard sayings" in relation even to our good human behavior. The contrast between God's ways and ours is sharp. For example, let us consider some of the Beatitudes as Matthew records them.

"Blessed are the poor in spirit, for theirs is the kingdom of heaven" (Matt. 5:3). The words which are translated "poor in spirit" may describe those who in their inmost hearts know themselves to be of little worth before the greatness and holiness of God. There is no implication of undue self-deprecation or of a cringing attitude. Rather this suggests the honest humility of one who knows that his best efforts fall short of perfection and that everything he does is tainted with sin and selfishness. This may be the basic beatitude. It speaks of the man who *knows* that God's ways are far above him, who knows himself to be a sinner. Such a man, while striving mightily to obey the will of God, can never consider himself, or his church, or his nation, or any human institution perfect. Probably only in this complete absence of human pride can the kingdom of heaven be approached.

"Blessed are those who mourn, for they shall be comforted" (Matt. 5:4). Mourning indicates a sense of loss. It
may be the loss of a loved one, but it may also refer to the
sorrows and disappointments which come with the loss of
cherished dreams or plans. When our human schemes succeed, we may become too self-confident. Perhaps only tragedy
and failure bring us close enough to God that he may
enfold us in the comfort of his everlasting arms. Success in
following our own ways, whether we be an individual or a
church or a nation, may be a complete barrier to God's way.

"Blessed are the meek, for they shall inherit the earth"
(Matt. 5:5). If poor in spirit in the first beatitude is the opposite of pride, meekness may be the opposite of arrogance.
The Interpreter's Bible has a telling description of the meek:
"They are not harsh, not self-assertive, not covetous, not
trampling in brute force. . . . Others claim their rights, but
the meek are concerned about their duties. Others are
clamant and advertise, but the meek walk in a quiet godli-
ness. Others seek revenge, but the meek 'give place unto
wrath' (Rom. 12:19). How the word must have cut across
the fashion of Christ's own time! The Jews asserted their
pride of race, the Romans their pride of power, the Greeks
their pride of knowledge, even as modern nations insist on
their 'place in the sun'; but the meek are content to walk
in the shadow where God keeps watch over his own."[1] Such
people, Jesus says, shall inherit the earth. While this may
seem at first as unlikely as any of these strange sayings, second
thought may remind us that even our human experience says
this is true. Force and violence may prevail for a time, but
gentleness and kindness win out in the end.

"Blessed are those who hunger and thirst for righteousness,

---

1 George A. Buttrick in *The Interpreter's Bible*, Vol. 7, p. 282. Abingdon-Cokesbury
Press, 1951. Used by permission.

for they shall be satisfied" (Matt. 5:6). Our human life is full of hungers and of desires. And we may achieve that for which we hunger! But how often have we desired something greatly, worked and sacrificed to attain it, only to find it not really worth having. God seems to be saying here, "Only as your desire in life is turned to me and to my will can you find true satisfaction." If we can want what God wants, we shall be satisfied. But his ways are not our ways.

And so with the others who are called blessed—the merciful, the pure in heart, the peacemakers, those who suffer persecution—none would seem, from a human point of view, to be the most fortunate of men. Yet Jesus says they are. And as we read on through the Sermon on the Mount, we find one example after another of Jesus' turning our usual human standards of behavior upside down. No wonder the leaders of church and state of his day could not abide his presence!

Are we any different today? Do not we, too, try to control our own destinies and the course of the world? Even in our church life, do we not seek to maintain our ways, rather than to find and follow God's will? It hurts our pride to admit that there may be a justice higher than our idea of justice, or a "good" far greater than any which we know. Like all human beings in all ages, we still want God on our own terms, in *our* own image.

As we turn back to the questions with which we started —the Christian faith has an answer. It says that there is much pain and sorrow in the world. Some of it has come about because of the rebellion and evil of man. Much of it is a result of our insistence on following our ways rather than God's. Yet, in spite of our rebellion, God loves and forgives. And his love has the power to turn human tragedy to blessing. He has promised us the kingdom of heaven. But we will come to this kingdom only by his way—not by our own.

The Mind of Christ

Have this mind among yourselves, which you have in Christ
Jesus.   —PHILIPPIANS 2:5

✝ PAUL WAS A GREAT psychologist. He uses terms translated
"mind" more than fifty times, such as "the mind,"
"mind of the spirit," "carnally minded," "spiritually
minded." When he was converted, he had an urgent intellectual problem, for he was a scholar. Being intellectually
honest, he had to bring his thinking into line with his new
life, the new way which had been so repugnant to him that
he at first persecuted it. So he went three years into seclusion,
in Arabia, to think, to meditate, in order to make his new
emotional experience harmonize with his thinking. The
result was that he emerged with a theology, a thought system
which has never been surpassed.

Paul had a clearer vision of Jesus than those who saw him
in the flesh. He saw Jesus with his mind's eye; he heard
Jesus with his mind's ear; and he resolved to follow him with
his whole mind. Twenty years after his conversion he could
say, "I was not disobedient to the heavenly vision" (Acts
26:19b), and he obeyed the vision until his death.

Conversion is a profound inner experience; it involves the

DR. R. R. WRIGHT, JR., Bishop of the African Methodist
Episcopal Church

mind as well as the emotions. Indeed, it cannot happen without a "change of mind." The Greek word most used for conversion implies a new mental attitude, a renewing of the mind, a new creation, being born again—not merely an emotional excitement. A man not converted in his mind, is not converted at all. Paul's whole life and his whole theology are illuminated by this text: "Have this mind among yourselves, which you have in Christ Jesus."

The words surrounding our text are significant: "If there is any encouragement in Christ, any incentive of love, any participation in the Spirit, any affection and sympathy, complete my joy by being of the same mind, having the same love, being in full accord and of one mind. Do nothing from selfishness or conceit, but in humility count others better than yourselves. Let each of you look not only to his own interests, but also to the interests of others" (Phil. 2:1-4). Then the text: "Have this mind among yourselves, which you have in Christ Jesus." And following the text comes this long dependent clause of over fifty words of explanation: "who, though he was in the form of God, did not count equality with God a thing to be grasped, but emptied himself, taking the form of a servant, being born in the likeness of men. And being found in human form he humbled himself and became obedient unto death, even death on a cross" (Phil. 2:6-8).

Paul stresses in these long and impressive sentences the quality of humility. The Greek word translated "humility" or "lowliness of mind," is not from the classical pagan Greek. The Greek idea and the Pauline idea differ widely. Consider the majestic portrayal of Christian humility. He, Jesus, humbled himself. Jesus was equal with God, with all the power and majesty of God. But all that was not a thing to be boastful of, or to be grasped at. No, Jesus "emptied himself, taking the form of a servant, being born in the likeness of men." No description of humility ever written is more powerful than that. Humility is the outstanding quality of Jesus' mind.

He humbled himself. No man humiliated him. When they put the crown of thorns on his brow, the purple robe on his shoulders, and slapped his cheeks, and spat on his face, they did not humiliate him. When they led him out to Golgotha and nailed him to the cruel cross, they did not humiliate him. No, he expected this, he deliberately humbled himself. And when he saw what they were doing, how foolish they were, he called in prayer from the cross: "Father, forgive them; for they know not what they do" (Luke 23:34b).

There was no boastfulness in Jesus' mind, no grasping for things; for his mind was geared to eternity. He had an eternal perspective, setting all things in their proper places. He saw the crucifixion in perspective, and knew its place in the plan of God. That is why he could say, "Father, forgive them."

Education is supposed to enlarge our mental horizon and extend our perspective. That is why we study history, literature, geography, and science. They add to our knowledge and to our humility—if we "drink deep." But the eternal perspective is given not by geography, history, or science. It comes from God. Only those who know God the Eternal, can have the proper perspective.

Most men go wrong because of lack of perspective, which comes from putting too high a value on themselves, thinking of themselves more highly than they ought to think. They cannot see the past clearly because of their selfishness; nor can they judge the present because their own self-interest is in the way and of course they are usually wrong on the future. For only humility can give eternal perspective. Humiliation comes to people who cannot take their minds off of themselves. Indeed, physicians say that one of the first signs of insanity is undue selfishness shown in blurred perspective. Many a man in high office has been adjudged insane because his office blurred his perspective. He really believed that "the king can do no wrong." Power ruins more men than it helps. For power puffs up little men like King Canute, and Emperor Nero, whom the devil made believe they were equal with God—the thing they grasped at.

Because of Jesus' humility he had no pride of race. He saw all men as God's children—as brothers, not underlings, slaves, sycophants, pawns. He could even see the divine nature in a sinner, whom he forgave, and did not stone. When the woman at the well, being asked for a drink, said: "How is it that you, a Jew, ask a drink of me, a woman of Samaria?" (John 4:9b), Jesus ignored the racial issue, put the question on the individual basis, and saved her.

Jesus did not boast of being a son of Abraham, Isaac, and Jacob; he was the son of man, the son of God. Jesus exhibited no pride of sectarian religion. True worship of God, he said, is neither in Mount Gerizim nor in Jerusalem, but "in spirit and in truth." Jesus had no pride of office. High priests, scribes, members of the Sanhedrin all looked alike to him. He humbled himself. As the "mind of Christ" possesses us we, too, become truly humble men and women.

Humility is not cowardice. Jesus was no weakling or coward. He castigated the leaders of his church, the scribes and Pharisees, when they were wrong; he called them hypocrites, straining out gnats and swallowing camels; he called them white-washed tombs. He faced the mob in the Garden of Gethsemane without flinching, marched unarmed through the streets of Jerusalem when he knew men sought to kill him. Humility makes you brave, not fearful and cowardly, for you rely on God.

Humility teaches one to put himself in the proper place. There is only one of himself and millions of others. Why should he crowd them off the stage and take the spotlight? "Let each of you look not only to his own interests, but also to the interests of others" (Phil. 2:4). True humility creates the ability to see the interest of others, and put your interest with the general interest, so that there may be fellowship of the spirit, like-mindedness, the same love, one accord, one mind! Jesus was never insulted because of anything done to him personally. He got warm when he saw others mistreated and dealt with unjustly. When he saw the temple defiled with the money-changers he turned over their tables. Men have no right to debauch the church to a money-making racket. When he saw influential men try to kill an exploited woman, though she had sinned, he rescued her. When he saw the blind, the lame, the sinful, he healed them, and took pity on them. He did not look after himself, but after those who needed him—the widows, the children, the poor. In his perspective he saw that the good of the one is brought about by the good of all. How few have this perspective today!

Nor did he fear men in high places. What did he say of one! "Go and tell that fox." Yes, the high and mighty in church and state hated Jesus and sought to destroy him. But we know today that the high and mighty knew not what they did. Selfish, arrogant, ignorant men in high places always misunderstand the humble, honest man, whether he be a Socrates, a John the Baptist, an Elijah, or a James, or some honest, humble man in a local church or community. Every man who properly understands his relationship to God must be humble. Only the fool is otherwise. Any man, who, because of his Ph.D., his LL.D., or his D.D. gloats over his knowledge, is a fool in the sight of God Almighty. Comparing himself with other men, he may be called learned, but as the psalmist said: "When I look at thy heavens, the work of thy fingers, the moon and the stars which thou hast established;

what is man?" (Ps. 8:3-4a) Only the ignorant can strut with haughtiness.

Men should make a habit of reviewing the works of God. This will keep them humble. The geologists tell us that the earth is over three hundred million years old. How old other planets and other systems are, we have no guess. But of these three hundred million years man has perhaps not existed one hundred thousand nor used his brains for thinking twenty-five thousand years. Yet God has been thinking throughout eternity! What is man, who lives but a flicker in the light of universal existence? What is the wealth of a man who owns a big farm, a city mansion, a dozen houses, a few thousand dollars of stocks and bonds, in the light of our Father who has riches untold? You see little men lord it over their fellow men, boast of their learning or their holdings; they are foolish, or they just do not have proper perspective.

Humility is that quality of mind by which one does not think of himself more highly than he ought to think, by which a man puts himself as one among many; a spirit that keeps him from grasping at things for his personal interest, and gives him a purpose greater than himself. The humble Jesus subordinated everything for one great purpose—the service of God and the salvation of mankind. "Have this mind among yourselves, which you have in Christ Jesus."

Jesus "became obedient unto death, even death on a cross." In all history we talk about Jesus' "sacrifice." But do you know Jesus hardly mentioned the glory he left in heaven; he put his mind on his mission to save. Sacrifice today too often means something material; giving up the larger for the smaller. We say, "So-and-so sacrificed a career in business in order to preach." That is the pagan idea. The old biblical idea of sacrifice is to devote something, or to give our best cheerfully to a high cause. There are many people who are always talking about their sacrifice. They do not express the mind of Jesus. When we understand that there is a greater purpose in this life than we now follow, and we give up the old small purpose for the new, that is true sacrifice, devotion, joy.

With the Christly mind it is a joy to devote ourselves to the good of others in any capacity, even to wash each other's feet. To the Christly mind it is "more blessed to give than to receive" (Acts 20:35b). Years ago a young woman taught Greek in a college. She married, and a friend saw her bathing her baby. The friend said, "What a sacrifice! Who would ever have thought you would give up a professorship in Greek to bathe babies?" "This is no sacrifice; this is the greatest joy of my life, and besides," she said to her friend, "there is more need to care for babies than to teach Greek, and take it from me, it takes more intelligence." That was true perspective, for in the last forty years most colleges have dropped the teaching of Greek, and many more have taken on the care of babies.

One sacrifices when he finds something large enough to absorb every effort of his mind, when he "loses his life in order to save it." For lack of a dominating purpose many people become neurotic or worse. They have not sacrificed, that is, devoted themselves unselfishly. Psychologists send people to church. I mean to say that the mind of Christ discerns the true significance of things, puts first things first, no matter what this costs in time, money, suffering, or even death, and enables a man to thank God for the opportunity to devote himself to the grand interests of the kingdom of God. That is what Paul did, and what we must do to realize the mind of Christ.

The mind of Christ is the mind of love. Jesus came to reveal love to the world, and thus to reveal God, who is love. Men had then refused, and still refuse, ideas of love. If you would truly know love, study Jesus, who revealed God's love.

And he commanded us to love God with all the heart, soul, and mind, and our neighbor as ourselves.

A current fallacy confuses love with sex. Love is greater than sex. It is that devotion of people which brings them into one mind, one accord. When Jesus says, "I and the Father are one" (John 10:30), he expresses true love. When the preacher joins two people in holy wedlock and the twain are made one, it is love. When Jonathan's soul is knit with David's, it is love. When Ruth says to Naomi, "Entreat me not to leave you or to return from following you; for where you go I will go, and where you lodge I will lodge" (Ruth 1:16a), that is love.

Love is complete forgetfulness. "Greater love has no man than this, that a man lay down his life for his friends" (John 15:13). Illustrating Jesus' love without lust is a tradition of Mary Magdalene, who, first at the tomb, exclaimed, "Rabboni," or "Teacher." Tradition calls her beautiful and bad. Before she met Jesus her idea of love was sex. Tradition says when her "lover" found out that she was following Jesus he demanded, "What is it that this poverty-stricken fanatic can give you that makes you follow him and hate me?" She replied, "Jesus has taught me true love, that I am an immortal soul, a divine personality. You love my body; he loves my soul. My beauty will fade, my body will shrivel, my health will fail, but my soul will live forever. It will go back to God who gave it. I will not leave him. I love him." Whether the story is authentic or not it shows the nature of love without lust. How many thousands of women are in the world who long for that love; and how many millions are disappointed when they find it not. Love is higher than sex. God is love; the mind of Christ is the mind of love.

The possession of the mind of Christ is not a thing of the moment. It must be cultivated. One cannot have overnight the mind of a physician, or the mind of a father, or even the

mind of a gambler. We must seek the mind of Jesus by cul-
tivating the attitude of love in little things, by worship, by
prayer, by study of the Scriptures, by witnessing, by meditation, by abnegation, by giving all, by self-discipline.

Jesus called his disciples but they did not all catch his
mind. He told them to tarry at Jerusalem. I wish I could
have been companion to those people of differing training,
temperament, and ambitions, together there. It must have
been a strain as well as a joy. But it was worth it for they
became of one accord, they had one ambition, the Holy
Spirit came upon them, and they wrought miracles. These
men came forth with one conviction, one purpose, humbled
before God, and unafraid of men. They possessed the spirit
of God. They were ready for anything. James and John no
longer strove for the temporal honor of ministers in a temporal kingdom. James was the first to give his life for Jesus.
John was found in a caldron of oil. Peter wanted to be crucified with his head downward. Thus the foundations of the
Christian church were laid. Thus the church has grown
through men disciplined in the mind of Christ.

In conclusion, let me express my heart's great desire, and
I speak now not alone as a bishop. Out of fifty years of experience in our ministry, the oldest active bishop on the
bench, ordained an elder before some of my colleagues were
born, let me like John of old say, "Little children, love one
another." "God is love. . . . If God so loved us, we also ought
to love one another" (1 John 4:8b, 11). Yes, love is the con-
summate flower of the mind of Christ. Therefore, love one
another.

Hitherto — Henceforth

Hitherto the Lord has helped us. . . . The Lord is round about his people, from this time forth and for evermore.
—1 SAMUEL 7:12b; PSALM 125:2b

✝ IN HIS BOOK *Philosophy of Religion,* D. Elton Trueblood declares that the shift in emphasis from ideas to events is a striking feature of the contemporary scene. He says:

Today the major tendency in Western religious scholarship is one which not only includes but accentuates the wonder of the story. Respect for the biblical message, far from declining as a result of literary scholarship, has grown remarkably in the recent past. . . . The renewed interest in the Bible has led to a heightened respect for the Hebrew genius, for the Bible is largely Hebrew in tone. Even the New Testament books, which constitute a minority, are deeply influenced by the Hebrew pattern and include numerous quotations, particularly from the Psalms, from Deuteronomy, and from Isaiah.

1 Samuel and Psalm 125 speak to us today as member

DR. MOSSIE ALLMAN WYKER, Minister, Disciples of Christ; Special Representative of the General Department of United Church Women, National Council of Churches

churches look back over ten years of organized history in the National and the World Councils of the Churches of Christ.

Hitherto the Lord has helped us. The Lord helped us when missionaries went all over the world taking the good news, the gospel message of hope and fulfillment. Their first concern was to share the life and message of Jesus Christ.

They established schools, believing that the best way to share the Book, and to help people help themselves, was to teach them to read and write. When they could read and write, they became articulate. The missionaries, from their own denominational backgrounds, trained and encouraged people in many ways, but they soon found, in the words of Bishop Brent, that "a divided church cannot save a sinful world." They realized that Christianity represented a minority group in the Orient and in Africa, that they must learn to work together and be ready to assume increasingly their roles as maturing persons.

Ecumenical discussions were initiated on the world level. Soon leaders were asking questions, and seeking solutions. What caused our division? How could we find unity in life and work? Our unity is in Christ. How can this idea be implemented in the life of the church and in the world? Finally, after the formation of the World Council of Churches had been delayed because of war, the needed action was taken.

In 1948 a large number from the United States representing our many communions assembled in Amsterdam, The Netherlands, with delegates from all over the world for the formation meeting of the World Council of Churches of Christ. We shall never forget the lengthy debate, and finally how a motion was made and seconded that the World Council of Churches be formed. There was then a hush over the entire Concert Hall as the presiding chairman, the Archbishop of Canterbury, called for the vote. One felt caught up in the onsweep of history as the much-discussed World

Council of Churches became a fact. We left Amsterdam with the words *"We intend to stay together"* ringing in our ears.

Within two years, in 1950, we witnessed the formation of the National Council of the Churches of Christ in our own country. In spite of Cleveland's worst blizzard in years, delegates arrived in sufficient numbers to complete the formation of this great organization. Many still laugh over the story of a group of Southern ministers going on foot, carrying their heavy suitcases through the deep snow to the hotels because no taxis were available. Finally one minister dropped his suitcase and stopped to declare, "I'm sure glad we didn't win the war between the States. We would have had to occupy *this!*"

The Lord helped us during the difficult days of formation. We came from varying backgrounds, different denominations. We did not understand each other; we quickly judged. However, we always felt the moving of the Holy Spirit in our midst, and yearned for unity in our witness. The Lord helped us not only to "stay together" but to "move forward together."

Pioneering days are strenuous; building a new organizational pattern is difficult; but perhaps the hardest test is ahead. We must now build a strong structure on the good foundation. We need to move from "hitherto" to "henceforth" and remind ourselves that "the Lord is round about his people, from this time forth and for evermore."

In 1955 an international team of four women was sent by the General Department of United Church Women on a mission of good will around the world. While in India the women interviewed a number of outstanding Indian ladies who are active in government and in civic life. As they visited with Mrs. Gandhi in Prime Minister Nehru's home, she explained that it has been much more difficult to rally their country's interest in building a strong self-governing nation (especially with the young people) than it was to win their goal in a revolution. The people never counted the cost as they struggled for their freedom, but now that they daily face the development of their new government, many grow restless and indifferent. She shared with the team information about the program she has helped develop with which she hopes to interest the young people in their own Indian arts and national culture.

We seem to have arrived now at this point in the National Council of Churches. The past decade has been filled with constant struggle, resentment, getting acquainted, adjustment, and renewal. Slowly, progress has come. Decisions have been made, sometimes at great cost, but under God the design becomes increasingly clear. Debate and free discussion have been a part of the General Board's agenda. The cross-fertilization of sharing beliefs and practices has helped to increase mutual appreciation.

If the ecumenical movement is right, it will continue to grow under divine direction. There have been many adversaries and much opposition. Ramsay MacDonald is quoted as saying, "Even a government of archangels would fail without an opposition." The National and World Councils of Churches of Christ have been beset and besieged, under constant attack by an opposition all along the way. The leaders of the Councils have not fought fire with fire. They have gone ahead with the work they believed must be done according to the will of God as they saw it.

The Lord will be round about his people—henceforth. Perhaps one of the greatest needs in the new decade is for interpretation at the state and local levels. While we have made tremendous progress at the national and world levels, there is much to be desired locally. Not only has there been little positive information given out across the country, but much *misinformation* has been "boomed" at the people from some of the pulpits, from the press, radio, and television. Many people who read and listen to attacks against the National Council of Churches do not have the other side presented to them and so they cannot make an objective judgment for themselves. At times, leaders connected with the National Council of Churches have had the privilege of answering questions locally about this organization at forums and luncheon meetings. They simply stated facts as they knew them, calmly and without hysteria or anger. People in the audience who had been convinced by other persons that the National Council of Churches is "atheistic" or "communistic" or some other "istic," have come up to thank the speaker for the information, saying they had never before heard this side of the issue presented.

It would be well if material giving the story of the National Council of Churches of Christ—who it is, and what it does— could be sent into every community across the country, and if ministers of the member churches could again and again preach on the unity of the church and the history of the ecumenical movement. It would be helpful if the National Council of Churches could provide for more persons in the field, who would be "ambassadors of good will" or "ministers of reconciliation" who could give the facts, and urge the people on to greater unity. They could come in at the invitation of the executives, administrators, or local pastors to give truthful answers and to build good will for the Church Universal.

The Lord will need to be round about his people—henceforth. Great unsolved problems and unresolved differences await divine guidance.

The church must increasingly witness in areas of rapid social change. It must give much thought to relinquishing leadership in the younger churches, and to have the humility to assume the role of partnership. We must lead our own country to a position of accepting people of all races as citizens and brothers, just as we expect the overseas workers to do as they serve in other parts of the world.

Little progress has been made in a deeper relationship of men and women in church and society. Women have been battling for equality of races, and the rights of God's children everywhere to serve as persons in their own right, yet they themselves are only beginning to achieve this for themselves. Few yet believe that a "woman's place" is where *she* can do the *best job*.

If Dr. Trueblood is correct in stating that "the shift in emphasis from ideas to events is a striking feature of the contemporary scene," and that "respect for the biblical message has grown remarkably in the recent past," then it is natural to expect that the ecumenical movement will increasingly claim the interest and respect of the church. It is built on the belief that Jesus Christ is divine Lord and Savior—and it is the great event of our generation.

Hitherto—and henceforth—the Lord is with his people!